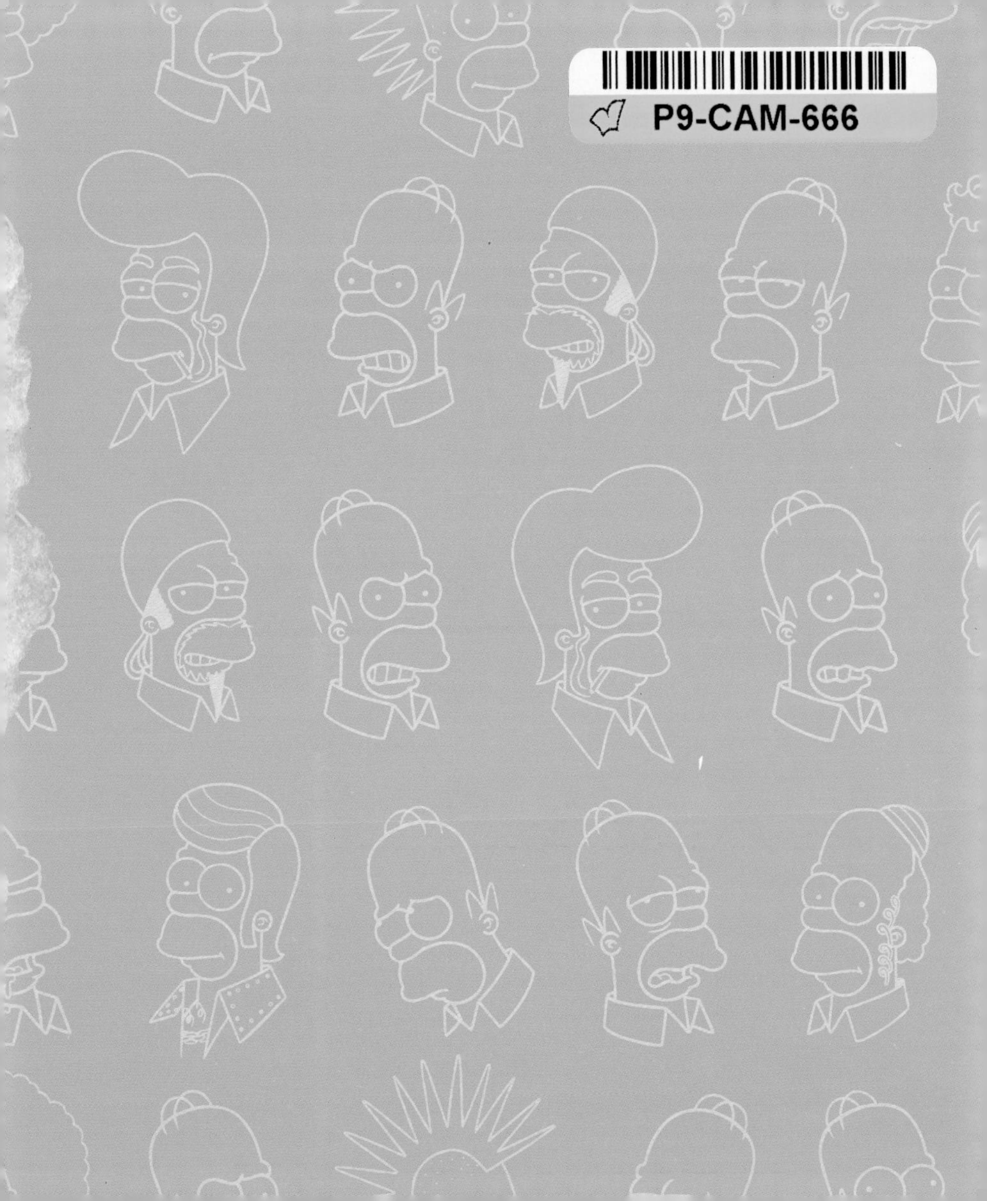

## THE SIMPSONS™ LIBRARY OF WISDOM
## **THE HOMER BOOK**

Copyright © 2004 by
Bongo Entertainment, Inc. and Matt Groening Productions, Inc. All rights reserved.

Printed in the United States of America.
No part of this book may be used or reproduced in any manner whatsoever without written permission
except in the case of brief quotations embodied in critical articles and reviews. For information address
HarperCollins Publishers Inc.,
10 East 53rd Street, New York, NY 10022.

HarperCollins books may be purchased for educational, business, or sales
promotional use. For information please write:
Special Markets Department,
HarperCollins Publishers Inc.,
10 East 53rd Street, New York, NY 10022.

FIRST EDITION

ISBN 0-06-073884-7

04 05 06 07 08 09 RRD 10 9 8 7 6 5 4 3 2 1

Publisher: Matt Groening
Creative Director: Bill Morrison
Managing Editor: Terry Delegeane
Director of Operations: Robert Zaugh
Art Director: Nathan Kane
Special Projects Art Director: Serban Cristescu
Production Manager: Christopher Ungar
Production/Design: Karen Bates, Art Villanueva
Staff Artists: Chia-Hsien Jason Ho, Mike Rote
Production Assistant: Nathan Hamill
Administration: Sherri Smith
Legal Guardian: Susan A. Grode

THE SIMPSONS™ LIBRARY OF WISDOM

Conceived and Edited by Bill Morrison
Book Design and Production by Serban Cristescu
Contributing Editor: Terry Delegeane
Research and Production Assistance: Nathan Hamill

Contributing Artists:
Serban Cristescu, Mike DeCarlo, Luis Escobar, Chia-Hsien Jason Ho, William Mahaney,
Bill Morrison, Kevin M. Newman, Mike Rote, Kevin Segna

Contributing Writers:
Jamie Angell, Scott M. Gimple, Nathan Hamill, Jesse L. McCann, Bill Morrison, Eric Rogers

HarperCollins Editors: Susan Weinberg, Kate Travers

Special Thanks to:
Pete Benson, N. Vyolet Diaz, Deanna MacLellan, Helio Salvatierra, Mili Smythe,
Ursula Wendel, and Doug Whaley

The SIMPSONS LIBRARY of WISDOM

# THE HOMER BOOK

Perennial Currents
*An Imprint of* Harper Collins *Publishers*

# Homer's TOP 40

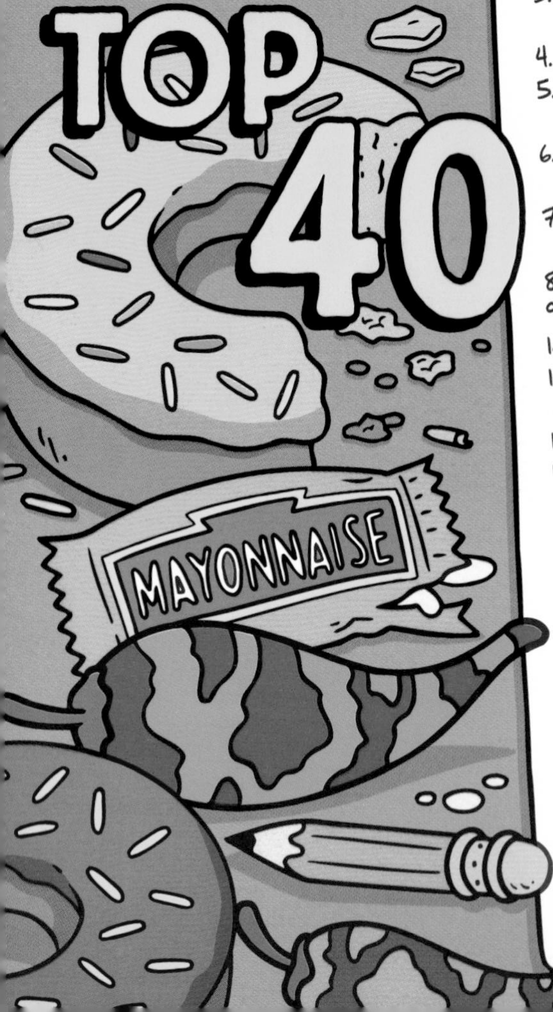
MAYONNAISE

1. Donuts.
2. Donut Holes.
3. Hot CHEESY-CRUST PIZZA, the Food of Kings!
4. "Big Ape Week" on Million Dollar Movie.
5. Four beautiful little words: "ALL-U-CAN EAT"
6. The lovely golden hue of sweet, sweet beer.
7. The hallucinogenic burn of a really fine chili.
8. Snuggling with Marge.
9. Beating the point spread.
10. Beating the middle-aged spread.
11. My patented, space age, out-of-this-world MOON WAFFLES!
12. Sleeping.
13. Napping.
14. Snoozing.
15. Lunch breaks with extra lunch in them.
16. The ovulicious flavor of fertility drugs.
17. "THE HOMER"—the car I designed for myself.
18. Bacon and its savory by-product, bacon fat.
19. Remembering Maggie's name on the first try.
20. The sound of pudding.
21. The wild bong-rattling fury of GRAND FUNK RAILROAD.

22. The bewitching variety of deli meats in a giant hoagie!
23. Can't-fail get-rich-quick schemes.
24. The gentle hypnotic swing of a hammock.
25. TELEVISION: teacher, mother, secret lover!
26. The sweet sound of Lisa's saxophone stopping.
27. The finest twelve and a half minutes of the day—HAPPY HOUR AT MOE'S TAVERN!
28. The cold side of the pillow.
29. The extra notches on my belt.
30. Any candy bar with the word "RAGEOUS" on the label.
31. The eerie peace you experience just before passing out!
32. The warmth and comfort of fresh underpants.
33. The crumbs at the bottom of the toaster.
34. Loving the family you're stuck with.
35. Greasy Joe's Bottomless Bar-B-Q Pit.
36. GREASY JOE.
37. Those little drinky birds that bob up and down.
38. Free mayonnaise packets at fast food restaurants.
39. The dank, musty beauty that is the bowling alley.
40. My top-of-the-line deluxe gas grill. (The one that says "Ned Flanders" on it.)

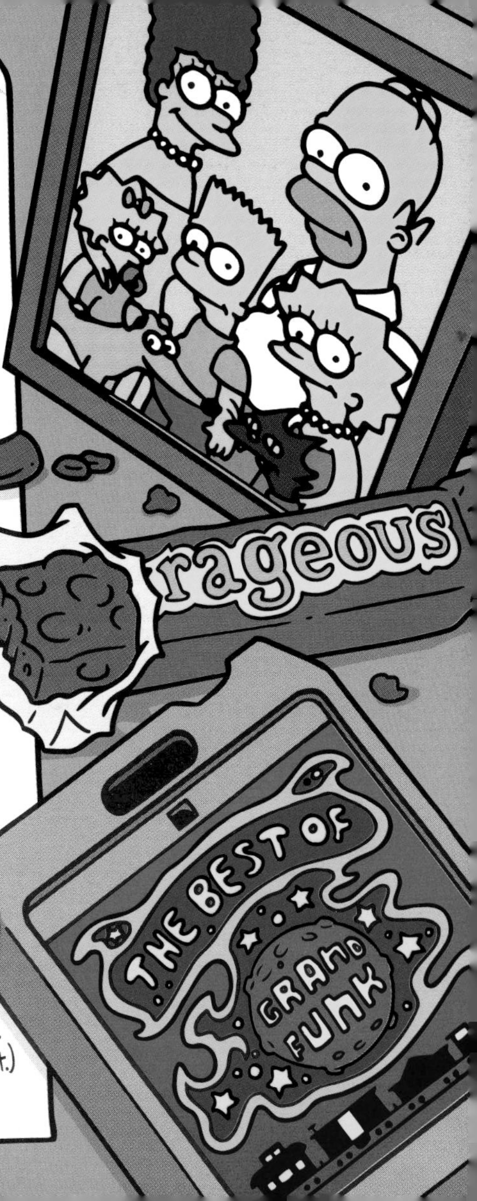
rageous
THE BEST OF
GRAND FUNK

# HOMER'S HISTORY

**AGE: DAY ONE**
Homer astounds medical staff/parents by somehow getting hold of pizza in hospital nursery.

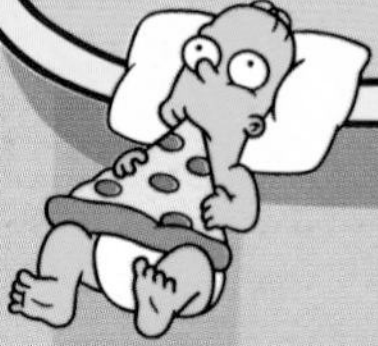

**AGE: 4**
Along with best friend Barney, Homer wraps his little red wagon around a tree. Boys vow to never drink beer again.

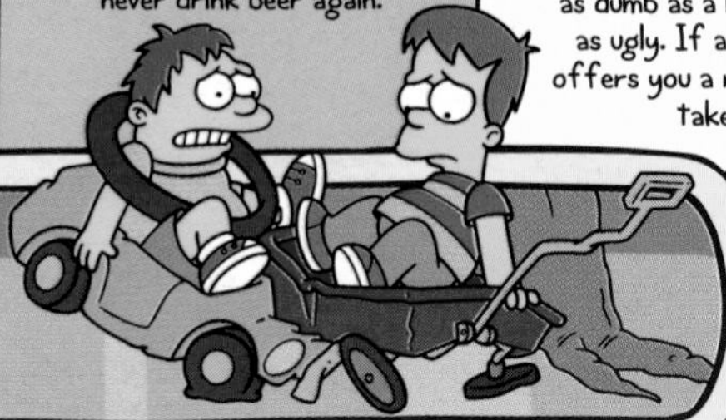

**AGE: 5**
Homer's first year of school. Never forgets father Abe's advice on first day: "You're as dumb as a mule and twice as ugly. If a strange man offers you a ride, you should take it."

**AGE: 6**
Homer invents new game that involves cramming crayons up his nose/sneezing them out. Accidentally leaves one lodged in his brain further lowering his mental capabilities. Doctors/teachers surprised that lower mental capabilities are possible.

**AGE: 7**
Homer plants hot dog tree behind family farmhouse; spooks the cows so they give sour milk; dreams of becoming president someday by imitating JFK. Abe inspired to start calling him "Melon Head."

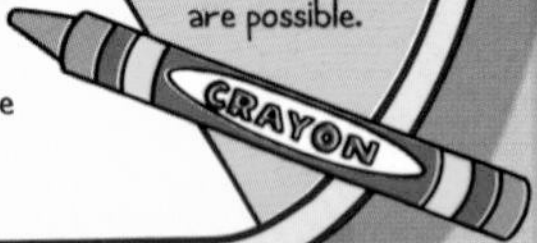
CRAYON

**AGE: 9**
Running from "the law," Homer's mother Mona leaves home. Told she had died, Homer spends night crying/mourning. Several evenings of Abe-administered NyQuil follow.

**AGE: 12**
Homer finds maggot-infested, bloated dead body at quarry swimming hole. Time it takes to suppress awful memory in crayon-impacted brain: 2 minutes.

**AGE: 13**
Learns about "birds and bees" by watching monkeys mating at zoo. At first, Homer thinks they are trying to kill each other.

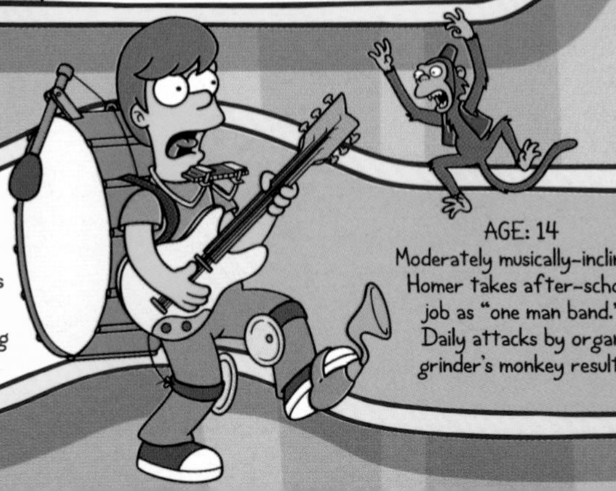

**AGE: 14**
Moderately musically-inclined, Homer takes after-school job as "one man band." Daily attacks by organ grinder's monkey result.

AGE: 17
It is "a very good year" for Homer to start drinking on regular basis. Tells Abe he is starting beer can collection.

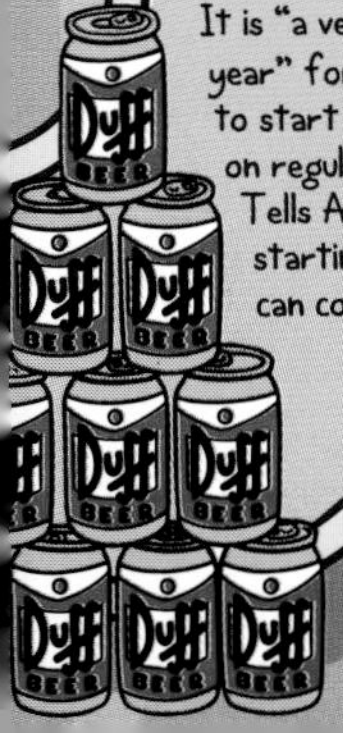

Duff
BEER


AGE: 18
Meets Marge Bouvier/they fall in love. After this Marge's father is never seen again. Rumors persist he was eaten by huge ape.

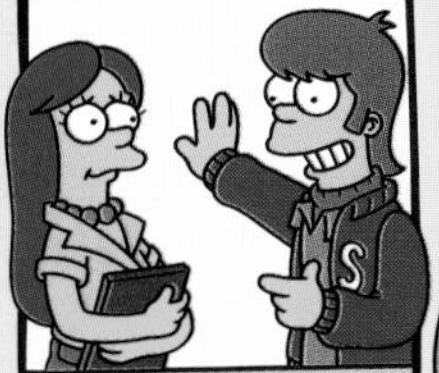

AGE: 21
Homer goes on "The Gong Show" with Barney; they receive more gongs than a break-dancing robot that catches fire.

AGE: 25
Homer/Marge marry after discovering she is pregnant. Realizing his miniature golf job is insufficient to meet needs of family, Homer tries his hand as candle maker/door-to-door knife salesman/attack dog trainer/Gulp'N' Blow attendant. Minimum wages ensue.

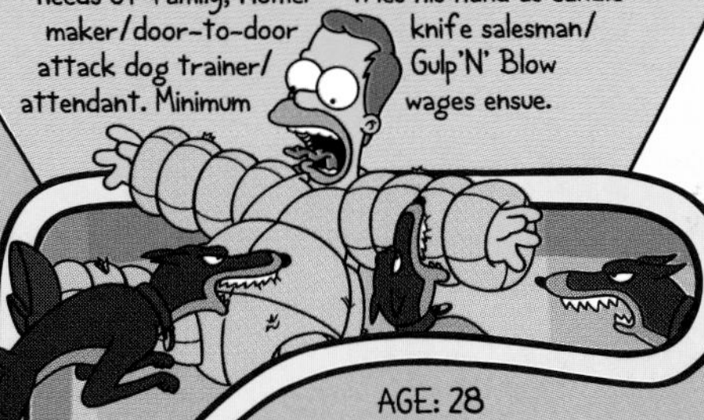

AGE: 26
Homer finally lands job at Springfield Nuclear Power Plant, changing life of C. Montgomery Burns forever. Shortly after, Bart is born, changing lives of everyone in Springfield forever.

AGE: 28
Homer forms barbershop quartet, The Be Sharps; writes award-winning song (Grammy® makes great back-scratcher). Lisa is born; combined household I.Q. increases dramatically.

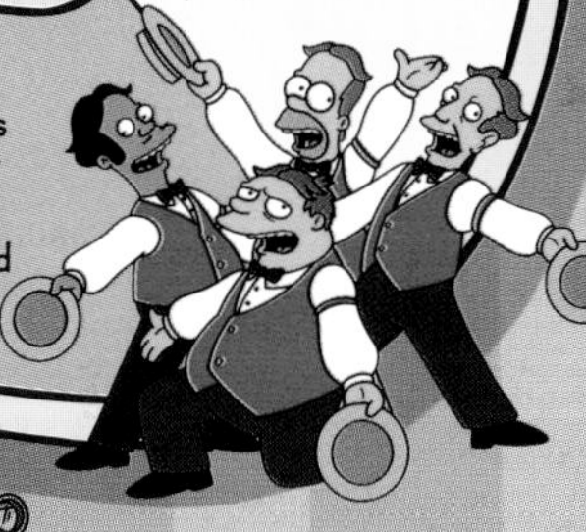

AGE: 31
Homer buys Lisa her first saxophone instead of using money for air conditioner during heat wave. Slew of heat strokes/saxophone-induced headaches follow.

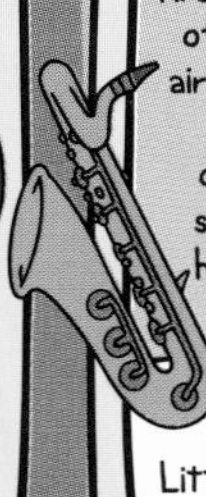

AGE: 35
Year of dreams: Little Maggie, "a dream come true," is born. Homer fulfills boyhood dream of eating world's biggest hoagie sandwich at county fair. He also accomplishes lifelong dream of running out onto field during baseball game, ruining pennant race dreams of Springfield Isotopes.

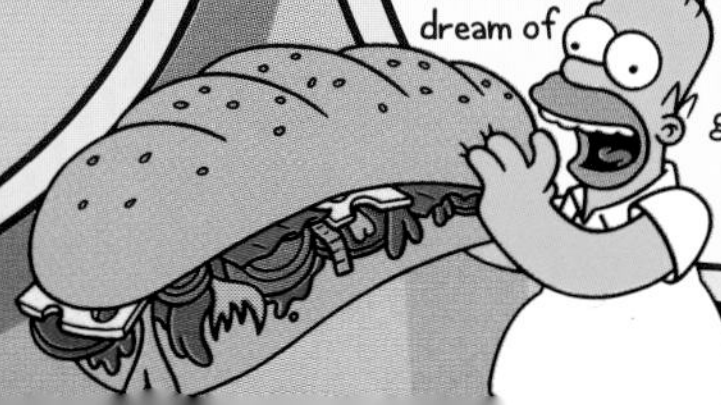

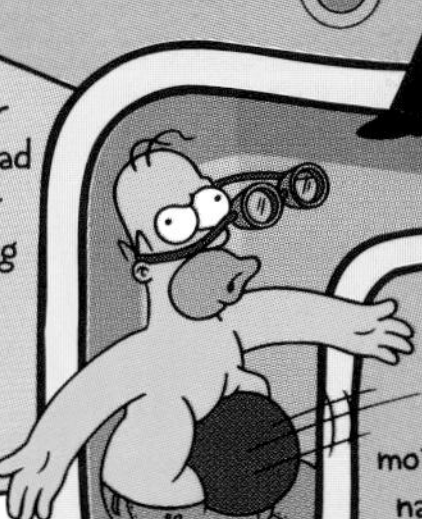

AGE: 36
Nothing matches 36th year: Homer learns his mother is still alive, his middle name is Jay; he has a half-brother, Herb Powell. He bowls a "perfect" game, takes several cannonballs to his gut, recovers from triple bypass, battles ex-President of United States, climbs Murderhorn. Nothing beats loving family waiting at home while in outer space eating potato chips.

# LITTLE KNOWN FACT:

The "J" in
Homer J. Simpson
stands for Jay.

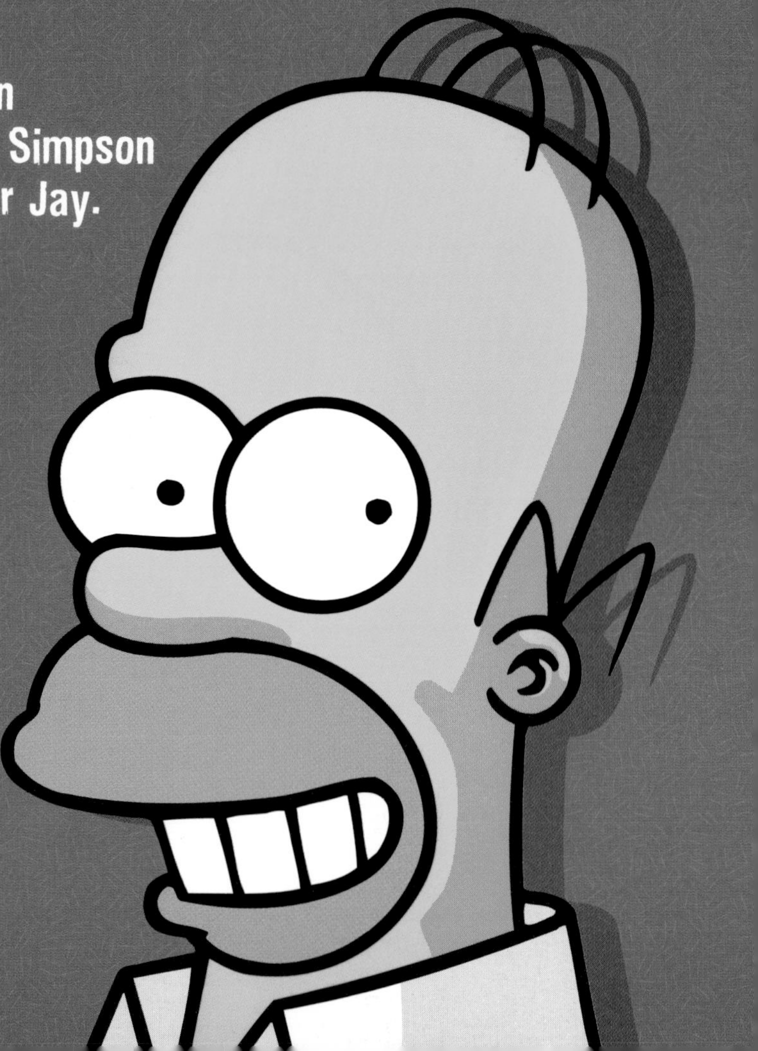

# Homer's Heroes
## COLONEL KLINK

As Homer's guardian angel, Colonel Klink appears to show Homer how miserable his life would be if he had married Mindy Simmons instead of Marge.

Who he is: Fictional German P.O.W. camp colonel from '60s TV series "Hogan's Heroes."

Identifying marks: Groove in upper left cheek from monocle.

Homer's obsession: Loves to taunt Klink with knowledge of secret antics by Hogan and his men.

True identity: Sir Isaac Newton.

Reason for charade: To appear as someone Homer would recognize and revere.

COLONEL KLINK! WHY HAVE YOU FORSAKEN ME?

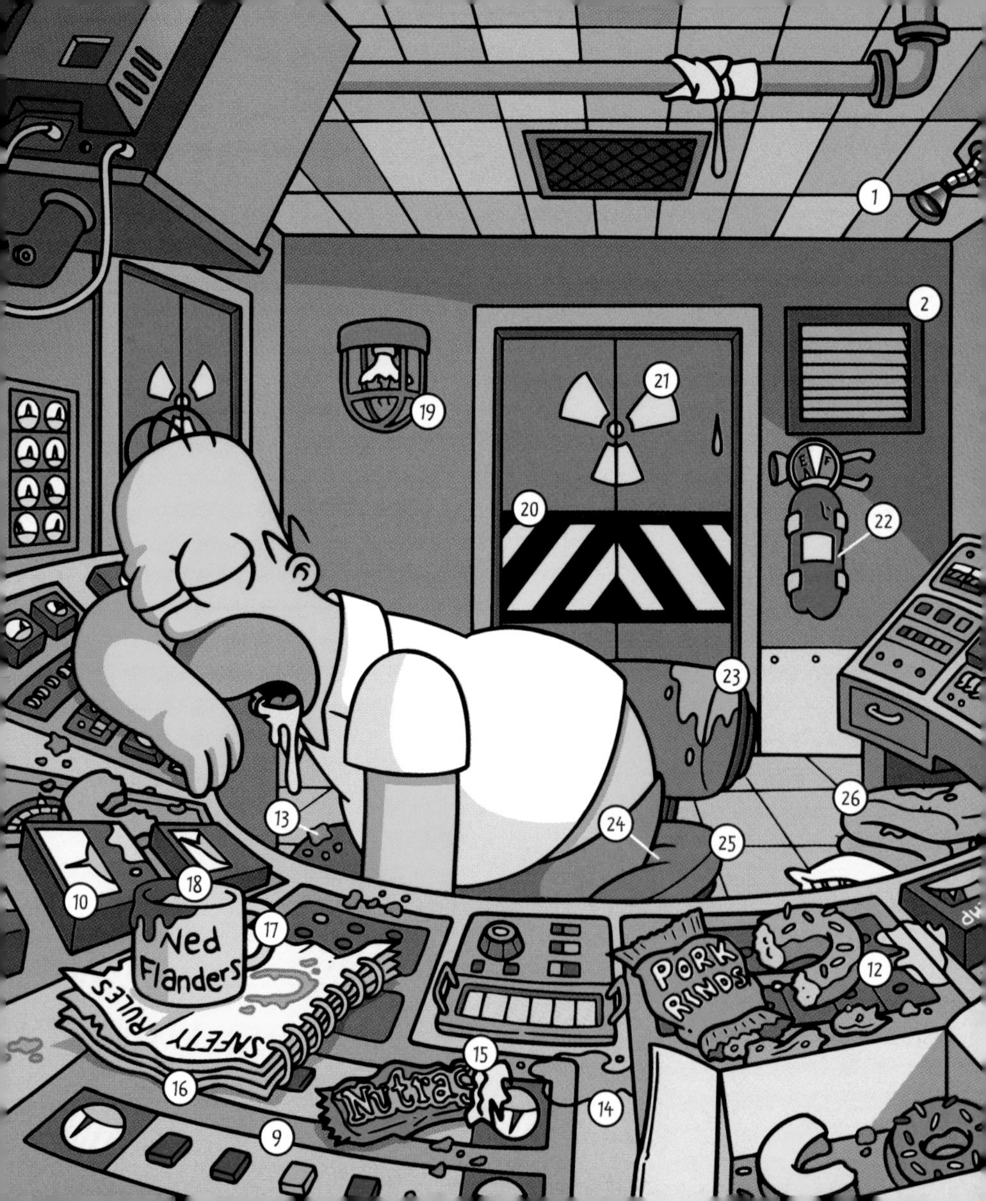

1
2
19
21
20
22
23
26
13
24
25
10
18
17
12
15
14
16
9
Ned Flanders
SAFETY RULES
PORK RINDS

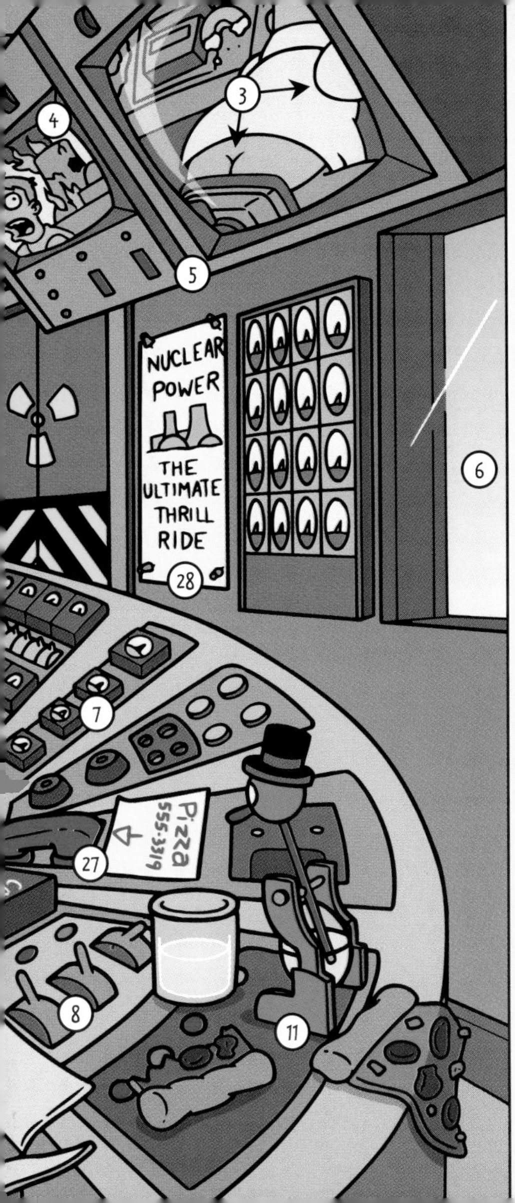
NUCLEAR POWER
THE ULTIMATE THRILL RIDE
Pizza
555-3319
1
2
3
4
5
6
7
8
11
27
28

# HOMER'S HAUNTS
# THE WORKPLACE

1. Mr. Burns' top-secret closed-circuit spying device.
2. Vent for dispersal of toxic gas.
3. Toxic gas.
4. Safety monitoring equipment.
5. Bewildering screens.
6. Freedom.
7. Distracting dials.
8. Confusing switches.
9. Perplexing buttons.
10. Mesmerizing gages.
11. Motivational device.
12. Donut.
13. Donut crumbs.
14. Coffee stains.
15. Candy wrappers.
16. Safety rules.
17. Coffee mug
18. Caffeinated sludge.
19. Warning light.
20. Access to break room.
21. Inscrutable symbol.
22. Vital safety device.
23. Uranium-enriched upholstery.
24. Butt groove.
25. Console chair with squeaky wheel. ("Nothing a little donut grease can't fix!")
26. Sleep station.
27. Emergency communication device with vital info.
28. Motivational poster.

# MR. BURNS HOMER'S BOSS

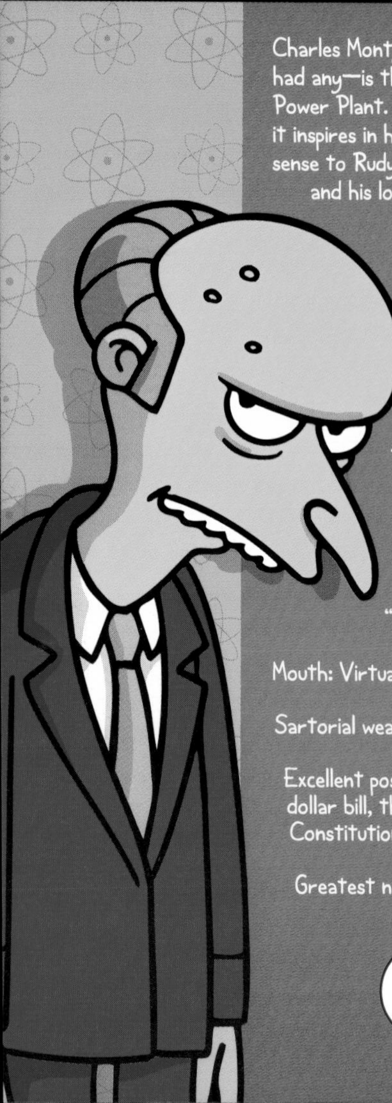

Charles Montgomery Burns or "Monty" as his friends would call him— if he had any—is the sole proprietor and evil overlord of the Springfield Nuclear Power Plant. Amassing immense wealth is his constant pursuit, and the terror it inspires in his fellow man, his true delight. Mister Burns credits his fashion sense to Rudy Vallee, his good looks to Dr. Jenkins Revitalizing Celery Tonic, and his long life to Satan.

Quote: "Cheating is the gift man gives himself."

Social Security Number: 000-00-0002

Bequests: Intends to leave all his wealth to the Egg Advisory Council, including his stock in Confederated Slaveholdings.

Weaknesses: Cashews, Gomer Pyle's singing voice, dodo eggs, Postem, and Bobo (his childhood teddy bear).

Intellectual pursuits: Penned a heartfelt book of poetry: "Will There Ever Be a Rainbow?"

Pets: Attack hounds, flying monkeys, the hairy denizens of "Tarantula Town," and his queen bee, which he named Smithers.

Mouth: Virtually smile-proof.

Sartorial weakness: The luxuriant caress of living fur.

Excellent possessions: Only existing nude photo of Mark Twain, a trillion dollar bill, the sword Excalibur, and a rare first draft of the U. S. Constitution with the word "suckers" in it.

Greatest nemesis: The Sun.

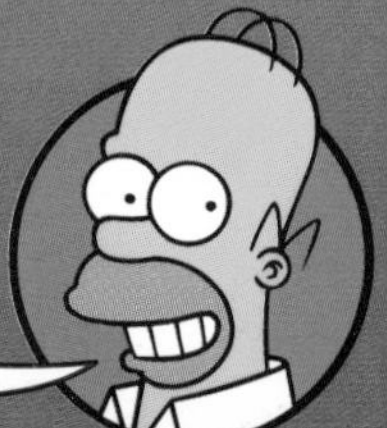
I'VE LEARNED A LOT WORKING IN THE SPRINGFIELD NUCLEAR PLANT FOR OLD MAN BURNS. THE EXPERIENCE MAKES ME TREASURE THE MOMENTS WITH MY FAMILY SO MUCH MORE.

Waylon Smithers is Mr. Burns' right-hand man at the Springfield Nuclear Power Plant. Whether it's pulling a rickshaw, moistening his eyeballs, or lying to Congress, Smithers cheerfully donates his time and services to his grandly exalted, highly esteemed, and strangely fascinating boss. If the situation warrants, he is also required to donate any needed organs.

Quote: "Mr. Burns isn't just my heartless money-grubbing boss, he's also my best friend."

Special skills: Bootlicking, ass-kissing, cajoling, wheedling, brown-nosing, fawning, flattering, soft-soaping, lick-spittling, kowtowing, groveling, belly-crawling, ego-stroking, truckling, toadying, apple-polishing, backslapping, butter-uppering, sweet-talking, sniveling, bowing, and scraping.

Most irritating responsibility: Reminding Mr. Burns of who Homer Simpson is.

Haberdashery distinctions: Bow ties, argyle socks, straw boaters, crisply pressed slacks, and natty collegiate attire.

Artistic pursuits: Penned a musical about Malibu Stacy, delicately rendered the indelible beauty of Mr. Burns in cray pas.

Claim to fame: Possesses the world's largest Malibu Stacy collection, including: Malibu Casey Stengel, Achey Breaky Stacy, and the rare Maliboo-ya Stacy and D.J. Plastic.

Occasional alter ego: "Snappy" the Alligator.

Heroes: Barney Fife, Paul Lynde, Jim Nabors, and Mr. Belvedere.

Political affiliation: Log Cabin Republican.

Allergies: Bee stings.

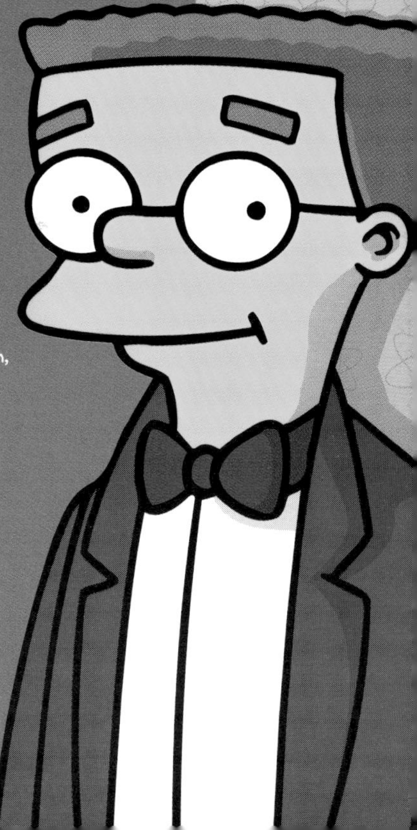

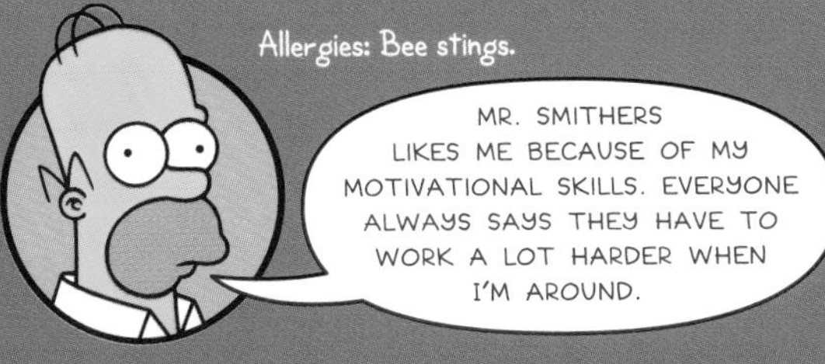
MR. SMITHERS LIKES ME BECAUSE OF MY MOTIVATIONAL SKILLS. EVERYONE ALWAYS SAYS THEY HAVE TO WORK A LOT HARDER WHEN I'M AROUND.

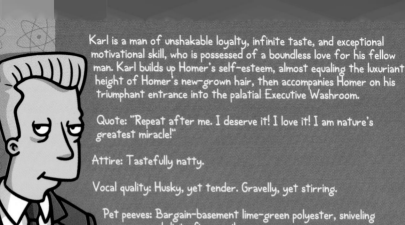

Karl is a man of unshakable loyalty, infinite taste, and exceptional motivational skill, who is possessed of a boundless love for his fellow man. Karl builds up Homer's self-esteem, almost equaling the luxuriant height of Homer's new-grown hair, then accompanies Homer on his triumphant entrance into the palatial Executive Washroom.

**Quote:** "Repeat after me. I deserve it! I love it! I am nature's greatest miracle!"

**Attire:** Tastefully natty.

**Vocal quality:** Husky, yet tender. Gravelly, yet stirring.

**Pet peeves:** Bargain-basement lime-green polyester, sniveling yes-men, and dirty fingernails.

**Turn-ons:** Breakfast in bed, strawberries and cream at Wimbledon, and gladiator movies.

**Friends:** Caterers, beauty salon operators, and the gals in the typing pool.

**The utility of wardrobe:** A man's suit should make him feel like a prince. It should cry out to the world, "Here I am! Don't judge me! Love me!"

**Secret to success:** Anticipating your employer's every need, even the need they don't know they need until they need it.

**Words to live by:** "Never kiss a fool."

WITHOUT KARL I WOULD NEVER HAVE EXPERIENCED THE SUBLIME JOY OF GOING TO THE BATHROOM.

# FRANK GRIMES HOMER'S BELEAGUERED FORMER CO-WORKER

Frank Grimes, 35-year-old Springfieldite, earns everything the hard way, but never lets adversity get him down—until he meets Homer Simpson. Homer's incompetence and nincompoopery drives Grimes into a sputtering, out-of-control rage. Imitating Homer, Grimes capers wildly around the nuclear facilities, madly chewing donuts, waggling his butt, and, finally, electrocuting himself on some high voltage wires.

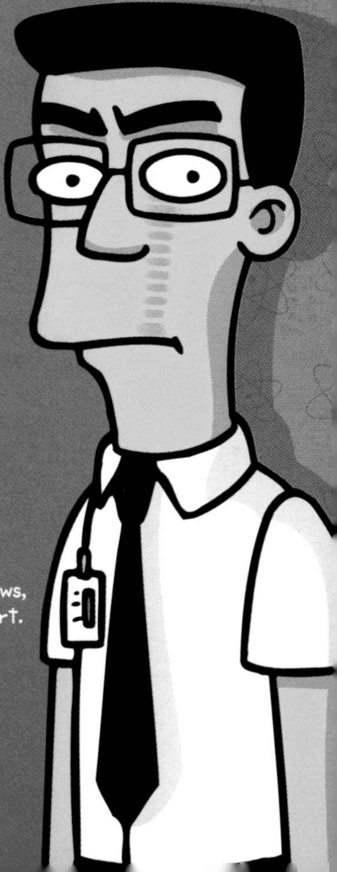

Quote: "I've had to work every day of my life, and what do I have to show for it? This briefcase and this haircut."

Education: Correspondence school degree in Nuclear Physics with a minor in Determination.

Extra shifts: Works nights at the foundry.

First job ever: Delivery boy (delivering toys to more fortunate children).

Shirts: Extra starch.

Pants: Extra creases.

Pencils: Personalized.

Daily provender: Packs his own special dietetic lunch.

Dwelling: A single room above a bowling alley—and below another bowling alley.

Previous brushes with death: Silo explosion, attack by crows, and the Seafood Surprise at the Springfield Squidport.

Despised nickname courtesy of Homer: Grimey.

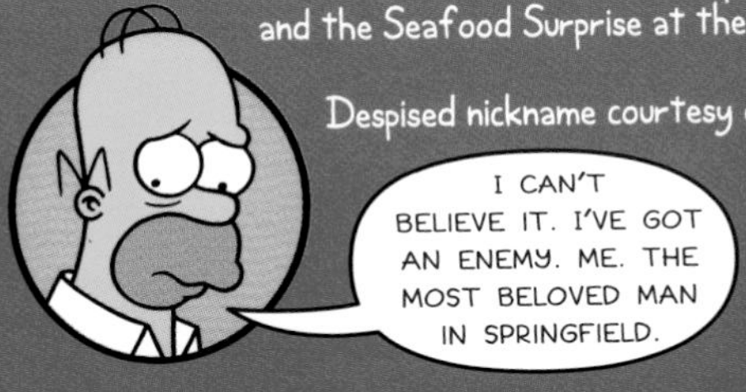
I CAN'T BELIEVE IT. I'VE GOT AN ENEMY. ME. THE MOST BELOVED MAN IN SPRINGFIELD.

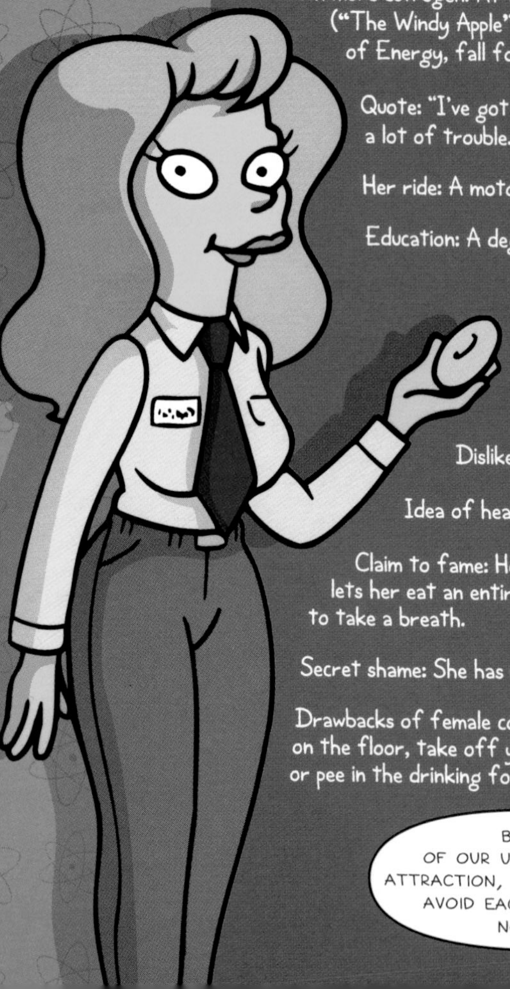

Crack government inspectors force Mr. Burns to hire at least one woman. He hires Mindy Simmons, who is like Homer in every way—except svelter and with more estrogen. At the National Energy Convention in Capitol City ("The Windy Apple") they are crowned the King and Queen of Energy, fall for each other, and nearly fall into bed.

Quote: "I've got a really wicked idea that could get us into a lot of trouble...Let's call room service!"

Her ride: A motorcycle.

Education: A degree in engineering or something.

Likes: Cheeseburgers, a quick nap before lunch, foot-long chili dogs, whipped cream straight from the can, raspberry swirl donuts with a double glaze, and broasted anything.

Dislikes: Exercise.

Idea of heaven: Drinking beer and watching TV.

Claim to fame: Her mastery of the art of circular breathing lets her eat an entire 20-piece bucket of chicken without stopping to take a breath.

Secret shame: She has no shame.

Drawbacks of female co-workers: Can't spit on the floor, take off your pants when it's hot, or pee in the drinking fountain.

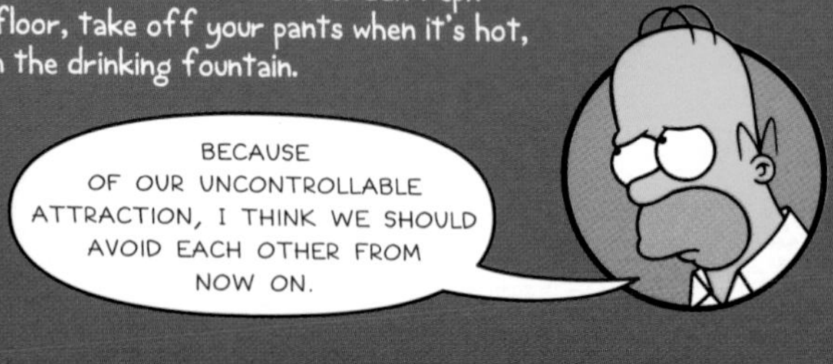
BECAUSE OF OUR UNCONTROLLABLE ATTRACTION, I THINK WE SHOULD AVOID EACH OTHER FROM NOW ON.

Categorized in their employment files as "fully replaceable cogs," despite holding Masters Degrees in Nuclear Physics, Lenny and Carl take comfort in the fact that they outrank Homer. Yet, they are united with him in their slack-worthy attention to detail, fondness for donuts, and ability to stretch a coffee break to the breaking point.

Quote: (Lenny) "Today's assault weapons have gotten a lot of bad press lately, but they're manufactured for a reason: to take out today's modern super-animals, such as the flying squirrel and the electric eel."

(Carl) "Everybody makes mistakes, that's why they put erasers on pencils."

Union affiliation: International Brotherhood of Jazz Dancers, Pastry Chefs, and Nuclear Technicians.

Sports: Bowling, poker, and the Springfield Nuclear Power Plant Softball Team.

Rankings in the Stonecutter Hierarchy: Lenny is #12; Carl is #14.

Shared antipathies: People poking holes in the jelly donuts, the high cost of stadium beer, and those good-for-nothing brainiacs of MENSA.

Infirmities: Lenny suffers from sciatica, while Carl has a crippling habit of telling the truth.

Strange if true: Bart once paid Carl & Lenny $1000 to kiss each other.

Turn-ons: Lenny likes bottle rockets, peering into peoples' homes, and practicing Ikebana, the ancient Japanese art of flower arrangement, while Carl likes to keep to himself.

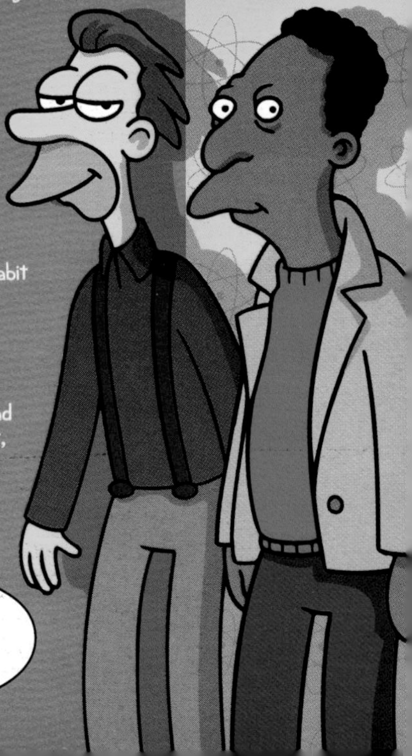

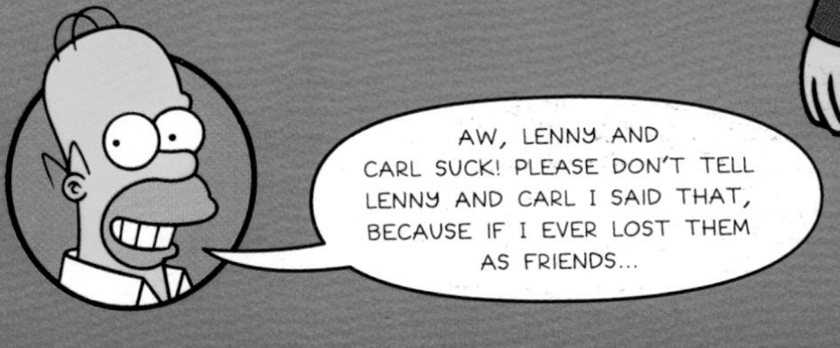
AW, LENNY AND CARL SUCK! PLEASE DON'T TELL LENNY AND CARL I SAID THAT, BECAUSE IF I EVER LOST THEM AS FRIENDS...

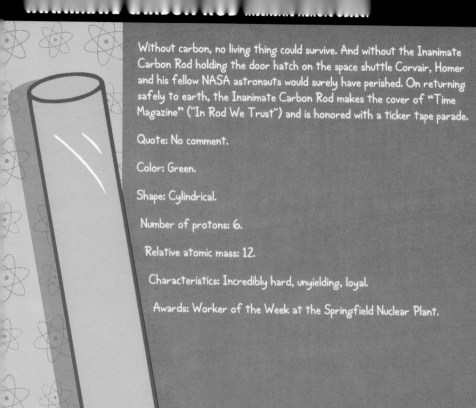

Without carbon, no living thing could survive. And without the Inanimate Carbon Rod holding the door hatch on the space shuttle Corvair, Homer and his fellow NASA astronauts would surely have perished. On returning safely to earth, the Inanimate Carbon Rod makes the cover of "Time Magazine" ("In Rod We Trust") and is honored with a ticker tape parade.

Quote: No comment.

Color: Green.

Shape: Cylindrical.

Number of protons: 6.

Relative atomic mass: 12.

Characteristics: Incredibly hard, unyielding, loyal.

Awards: Worker of the Week at the Springfield Nuclear Plant.

STUPID CARBON ROD! IT'S ALL JUST A POPULARITY CONTEST.

# LITTLE KNOWN FACT:

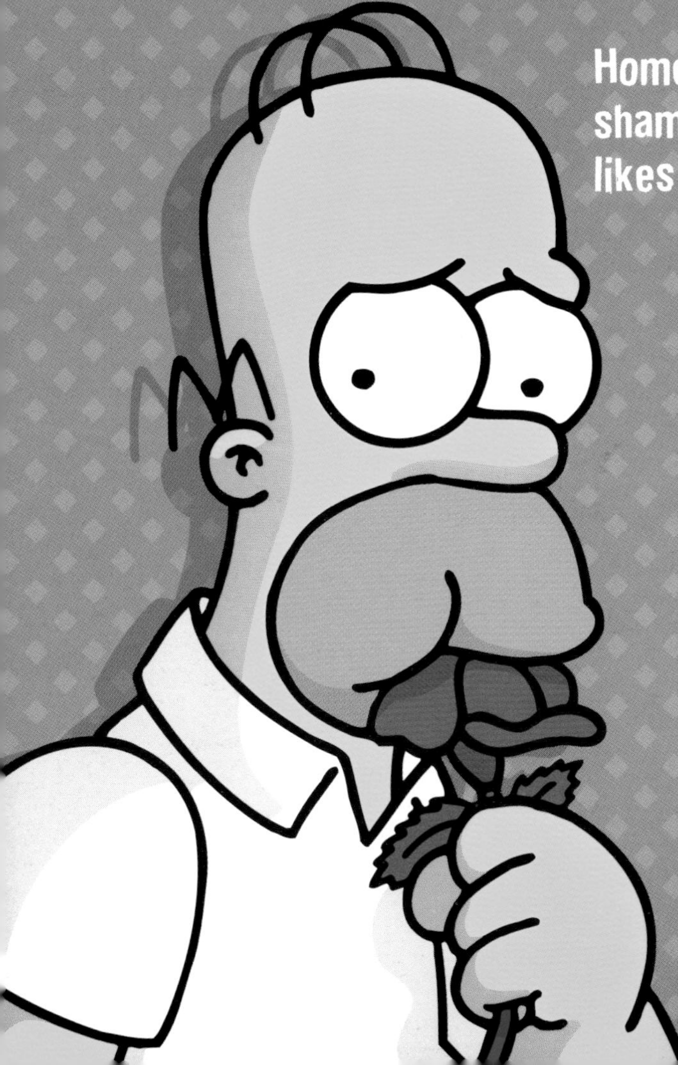

Homer's secret shame is that he likes to eat flowers.

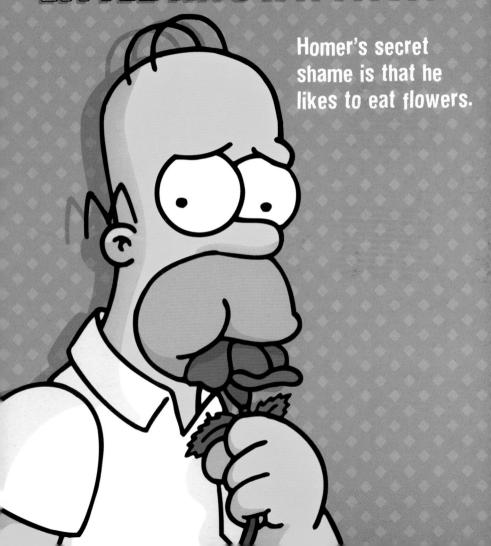

# Jerk of All Trades

## Homer Simpson's Rezoomay

Dear Potential Employer,

My current job as safety inspector at the Springfield Nuclear Power Plant affords me lots of time to pursue other occupations. Here is a list of jobs I have held in the not too distant past. Most, if not all, ended neatly with no lasting consequences.

Sincerely,
Homer J. Simpson

- Capital City Capitals Baseball Team Mascot (Dancing Homer)
- Shopping Mall Santa
- Car Designer
- Kwik-E-Mart Employee - Graveyard Shift
- Olde Springfield Towne Guide (Candle Maker)
- Slash-Co Knives Salesman
- The Pitiless Pup Attack Dog School Dummy
- Gulp 'N' Blow Employee
- Astronaut
- Manager of country music singer Lurleen Lumpkin
- Snow Plow owner/operator Mr. Plow
- Monorail Conductor
- Power Plant Union Representative
- "The Be-Sharps" Barbershop Quartet Member
- Student (Springfield University)
- Blackjack Dealer
- Personal Assistant to C. Montgomery Burns
- Adult Education Teacher
- Sugar Salesman
- Barney's Bowl-O-Rama Employee
- Krusty the Clown Impersonator
- Electronic Solicitor (Via Telephone Autodialer)

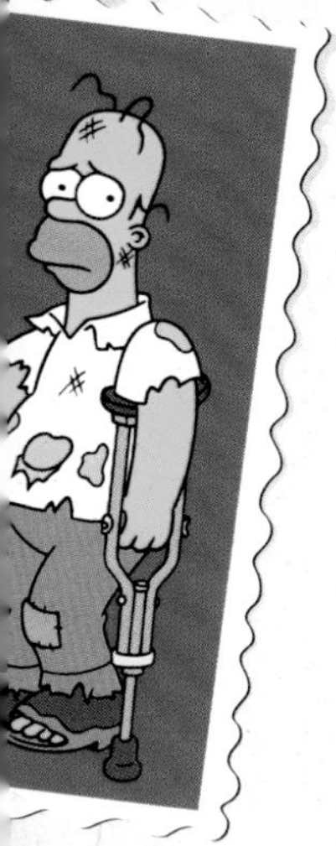

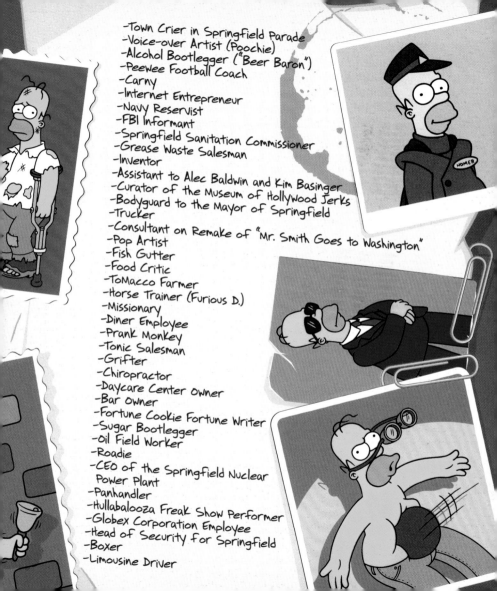

- Town Crier in Springfield Parade
- Voice-over Artist (Poochie)
- Alcohol Bootlegger ("Beer Baron")
- Peewee Football Coach
- Carny
- Internet Entrepreneur
- Navy Reservist
- FBI Informant
- Springfield Sanitation Commissioner
- Grease Waste Salesman
- Inventor
- Assistant to Alec Baldwin and Kim Basinger
- Curator of the Museum of Hollywood Jerks
- Bodyguard to the Mayor of Springfield
- Trucker
- Consultant on Remake of "Mr. Smith Goes to Washington"
- Pop Artist
- Fish Gutter
- Food Critic
- ToMacco Farmer
- Horse Trainer (Furious D.)
- Missionary
- Diner Employee
- Prank Monkey
- Tonic Salesman
- Grifter
- Chiropractor
- Daycare Center Owner
- Bar Owner
- Fortune Cookie Fortune Writer
- Sugar Bootlegger
- Oil Field Worker
- Roadie
- CEO of the Springfield Nuclear Power Plant
- Panhandler
- Hullabalooza Freak Show Performer
- Globex Corporation Employee
- Head of Security for Springfield
- Boxer
- Limousine Driver

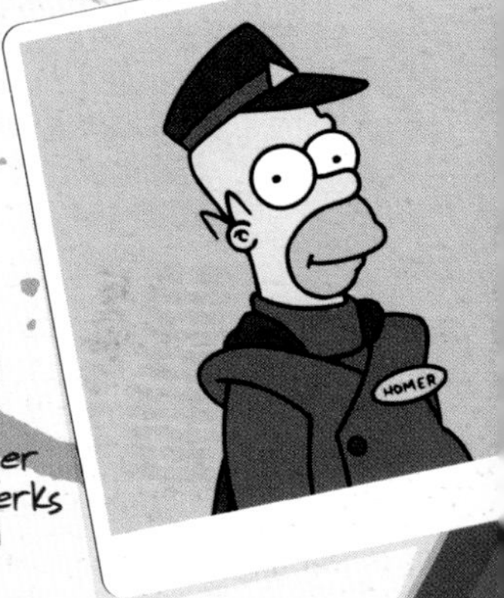
HOMER

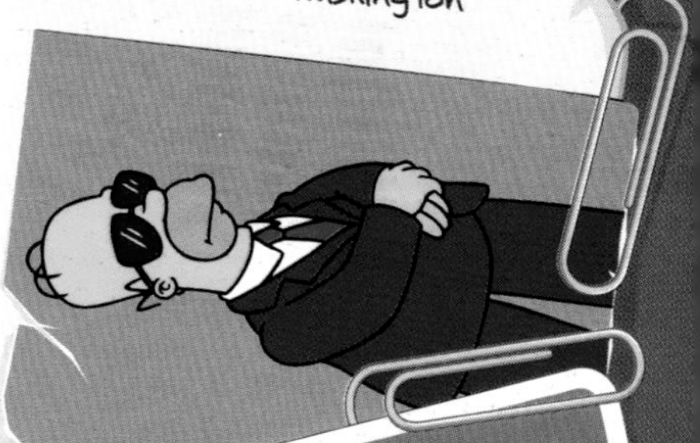

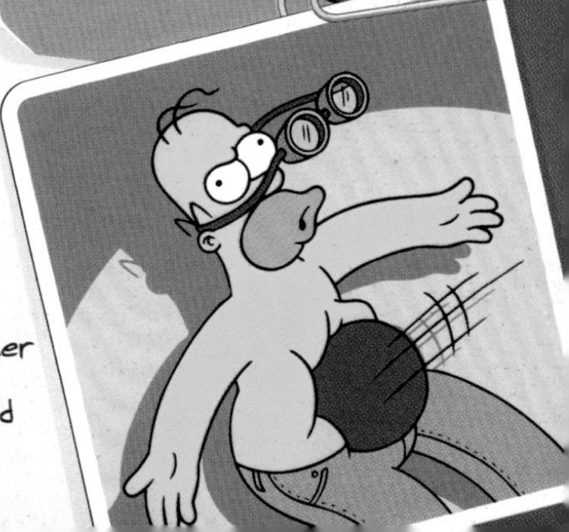

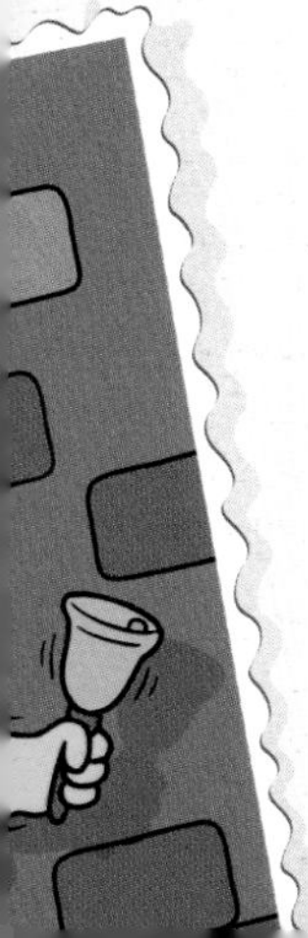

# THE ANATOMY OF HOMER

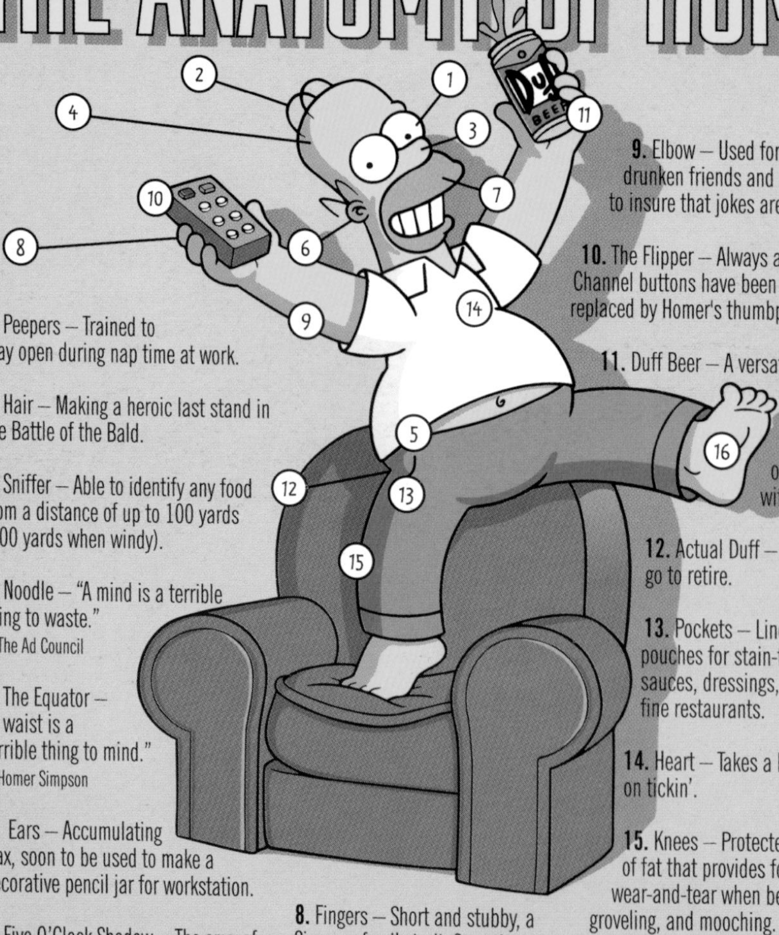

Duff
BEER
1
2
3
4
5
6
7
8
9
10
11
12
13
14
15
16


**1.** Peepers – Trained to stay open during nap time at work.

**2.** Hair – Making a heroic last stand in the Battle of the Bald.

**3.** Sniffer – Able to identify any food from a distance of up to 100 yards (300 yards when windy).

**4.** Noodle – "A mind is a terrible thing to waste."
– The Ad Council

**5.** The Equator – "A waist is a terrible thing to mind."
– Homer Simpson

**6.** Ears – Accumulating wax, soon to be used to make a decorative pencil jar for workstation.

**7.** Five O'Clock Shadow – The envy of George Michael and pouty male models the world over.

**8.** Fingers – Short and stubby, a Simpson family trait. Sometimes mistaken for sausages at breakfast and nibbled on.

**9.** Elbow – Used for jabbing ribs of drunken friends and strangers to insure that jokes are understood.

**10.** The Flipper – Always at the ready. Channel buttons have been worn away, replaced by Homer's thumbprint.

**11.** Duff Beer – A versatile brew. Accessorizes nicely with jeans and a casual shirt or boxers and a wife-beater.

**12.** Actual Duff – Where trans fats go to retire.

**13.** Pockets – Lined with plastic pouches for stain-free smuggling of sauces, dressings, and dips from fine restaurants.

**14.** Heart – Takes a lickin' and keeps on tickin'.

**15.** Knees – Protected by extra layer of fat that provides for unlimited wear-and-tear when begging, praying, groveling, and mooching.

**16.** Dogs – Always barking. Last seen by Homer (while standing) in the spring of '81.

# WHAT'S ON HOMER'S MIND?

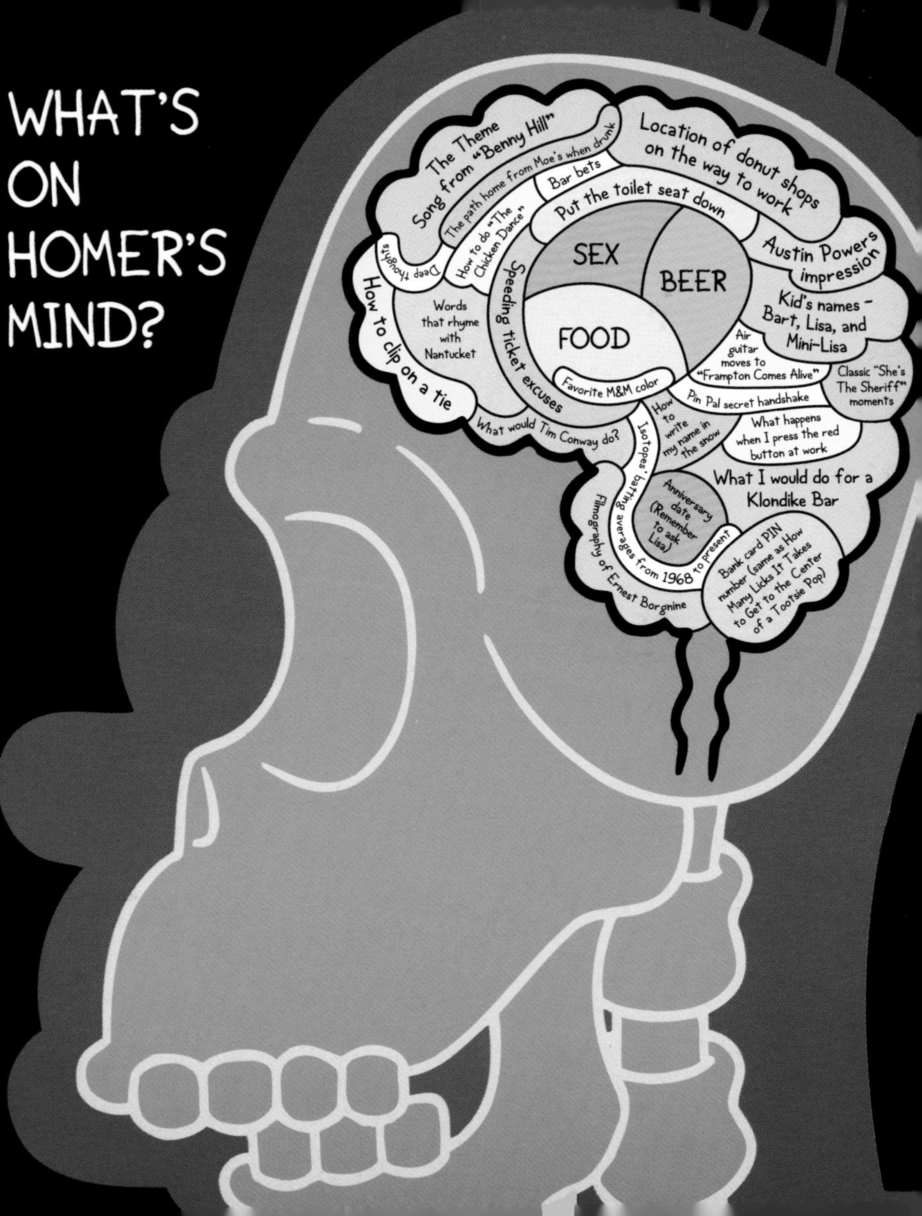

The Theme Song from "Benny Hill"
Location of donut shops on the way to work
The path home from Moe's when drunk
Bar bets
Put the toilet seat down
Deep thoughts
How to do "The Chicken Dance"
Speeding ticket excuses
SEX
BEER
FOOD
Austin Powers impression
Kid's names - Bart, Lisa, and Mini-Lisa
How to clip on a tie
Words that rhyme with Nantucket
Air guitar moves to "Frampton Comes Alive"
Favorite M&M color
Classic "She's The Sheriff" moments
Pin Pal secret handshake
What would Tim Conway do?
How to write my name in the snow
What happens when I press the red button at work
Isotopes' batting averages from 1968 to present
What I would do for a Klondike Bar
Anniversary date (Remember to ask Lisa)
Filmography of Ernest Borgnine
Bank card PIN number (same as How Many Licks It Takes to Get to the Center of a Tootsie Pop)

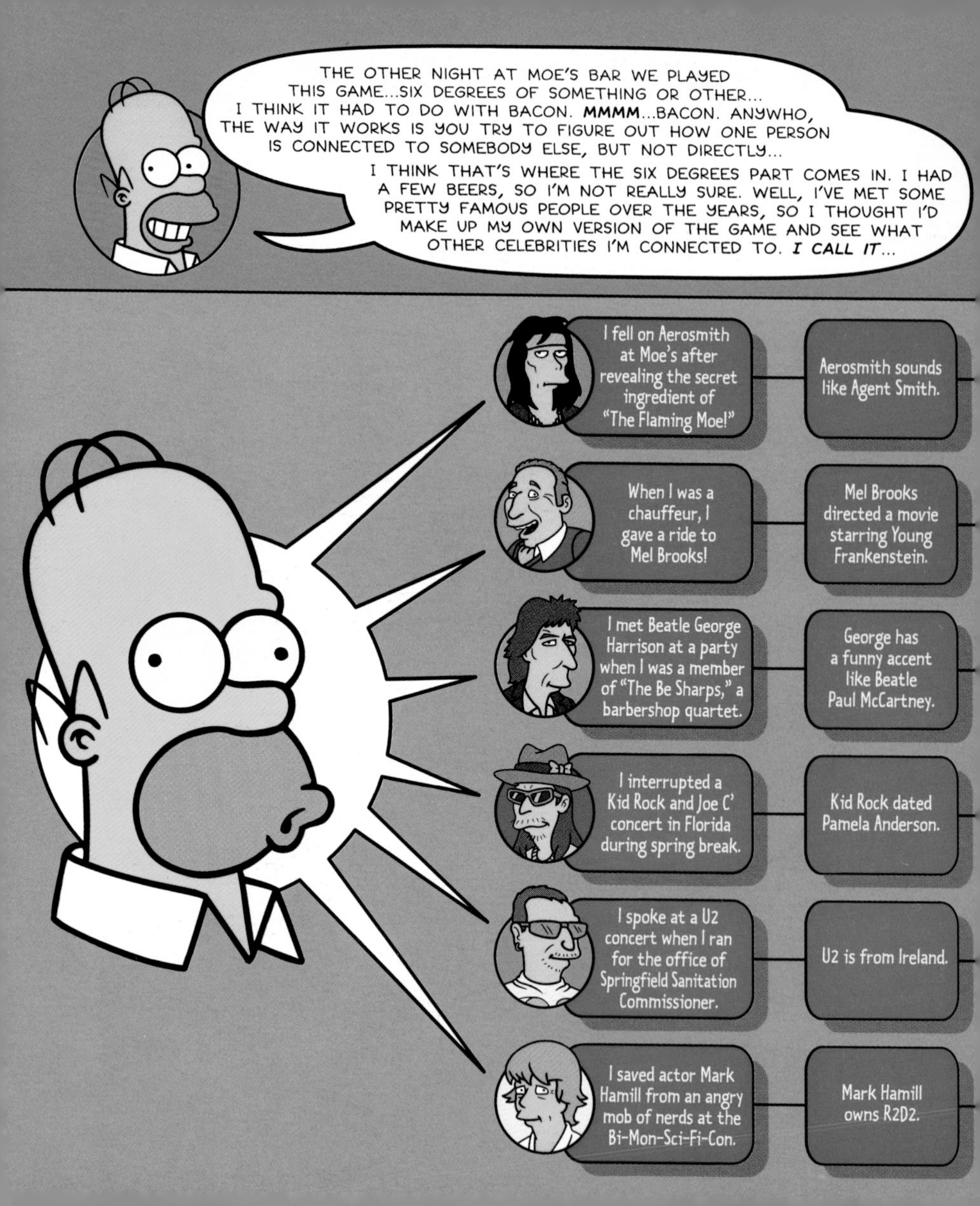
THE OTHER NIGHT AT MOE'S BAR WE PLAYED THIS GAME...SIX DEGREES OF SOMETHING OR OTHER... I THINK IT HAD TO DO WITH BACON. **MMMM**...BACON. ANYWHO, THE WAY IT WORKS IS YOU TRY TO FIGURE OUT HOW ONE PERSON IS CONNECTED TO SOMEBODY ELSE, BUT NOT DIRECTLY... I THINK THAT'S WHERE THE SIX DEGREES PART COMES IN. I HAD A FEW BEERS, SO I'M NOT REALLY SURE. WELL, I'VE MET SOME PRETTY FAMOUS PEOPLE OVER THE YEARS, SO I THOUGHT I'D MAKE UP MY OWN VERSION OF THE GAME AND SEE WHAT OTHER CELEBRITIES I'M CONNECTED TO. ***I CALL IT***...
I fell on Aerosmith at Moe's after revealing the secret ingredient of "The Flaming Moe!"
Aerosmith sounds like Agent Smith.
When I was a chauffeur, I gave a ride to Mel Brooks!
Mel Brooks directed a movie starring Young Frankenstein.
I met Beatle George Harrison at a party when I was a member of "The Be Sharps," a barbershop quartet.
George has a funny accent like Beatle Paul McCartney.
I interrupted a Kid Rock and Joe C' concert in Florida during spring break.
Kid Rock dated Pamela Anderson.
I spoke at a U2 concert when I ran for the office of Springfield Sanitation Commissioner.
U2 is from Ireland.
I saved actor Mark Hamill from an angry mob of nerds at the Bi-Mon-Sci-Fi-Con.
Mark Hamill owns R2D2.

# ...SIX DEGREES OF HOMER SIMPSON...sort of!

| | | | |
|---|---|---|---|
| Agent Smith starred in "The Matrix" with Keanu Reeves. | Keanu Reeves was in "Speed" with Dennis Hopper. | Dennis Hopper has the same name as Hopper from that cartoon "A Bug's Life." | Hopper is a bug that hops, just like Jiminy Cricket!  |
| Young Frankenstein was related to Regular Frankenstein. | Regular Frankenstein starred in a film with Bud Abbott. | Bud Abbott was half of a comedy team with Lou Costello. | Lou Costello was probably related to New Wave rocker Elvis Costello!  |
| Paul gave a vegetarian recipe to Apu, manager of the Kwik-E-Mart. | Apu's job was temporarily taken by actor James Woods. | James Woods starred in "Any Given Sunday" with Al Pacino. | Al Pacino sounds like Cappuccino. Mmmm...Cappuccino!  |
| Pamela Anderson starred in "Baywatch" with David Hasselhoff... | ...who starred in "Knightrider" with K.I.T.T. | K.I.T.T. is a crime-fighting vehicle not unlike The Mystery Machine from "Scooby-Doo." | Scooby-Doo jumped the shark with the addition of child star Scrappy-Doo!  |
| Ireland is famous for exporting Lucky Charms cereal... | ...which are hoarded by a leprechaun, similar to the one from "Leprechaun: The Movie" | "Leprechaun: The Movie" starred Jennifer Aniston. | Jennifer Aniston co-starred on "Friends" with Marcel the monkey.  |
| R2D2 was directed by George Lucas in the movie "Star Wars." | George Lucas dated singer Linda Ronstadt. | Linda Ronstadt did a Plow King commercial with Barney Gumble. | Barney is the bosom buddy of me, Homer Simpson!  |

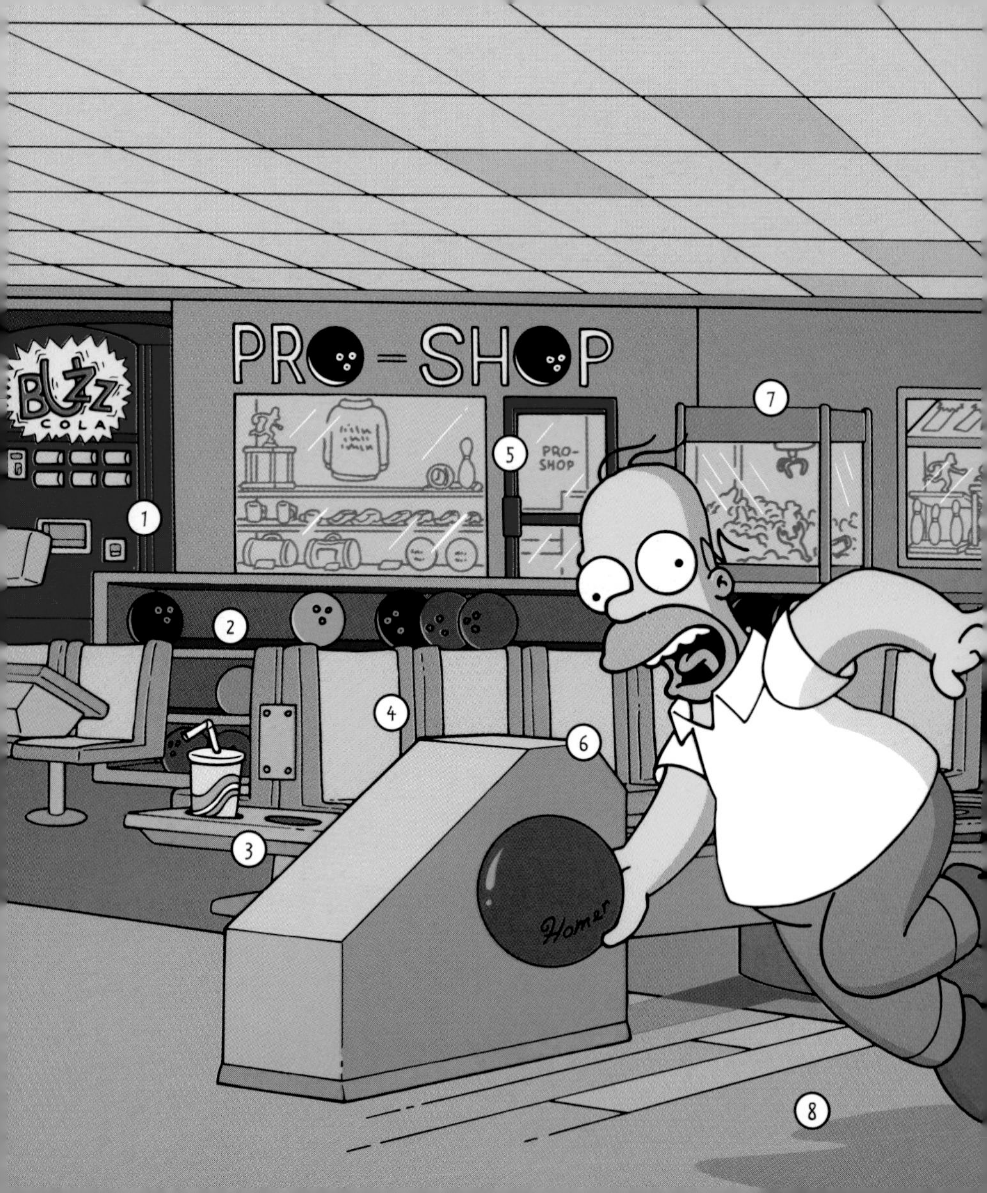

BUZZ
COLA
PRO-SHOP
PRO-
SHOP
Homer
1
2
3
4
5
6
7
8

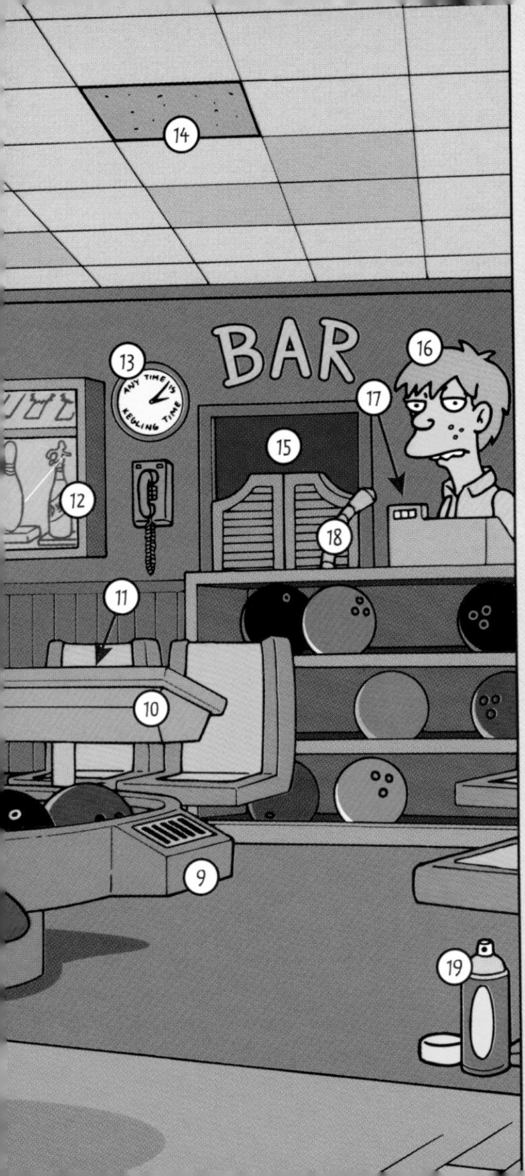
BAR
ANY TIME IS KEGLING TIME
14
13
16
17
15
12
18
11
10
9
19

# HOMER'S HAUNTS

# BOWL-A-RAMA

1. Energy supply.
2. Ball racks with bowling balls—"Prepare to commence hurling!"
3. Large beverage cup holders.
4. Luxurious, hard plastic, on-deck, banquette-style seats.
5. Pro-Shop entrance—"Look like a pro instantly without all that tiresome practicing!"
6. Standard issue hand-crippling device.
7. Novelty Claw Prize machine (features cute plush animals, kazoos, magic tricks, lobster harmonicas, and Harvard diplomas).
8. Floor surfaces (by the bar: sticky; on the lanes: slicky).
9. Sweat-B-Gone Mystery Air Blower 3000.
10. Scoring table.
11. Free pencils with scorecards.
12. Trophy case.
13. Clock—"Any Time is Kegling Time!"
14. Trap door in ceiling—holds "300 game" celebratory balloon.
15. Entrance to "The Eleventh Frame."
16. Courteous well-trained staff.
17. Dusty shoe rental cubbyholes (behind front counter).
18. Intercom microphone set to maximum distortion.
19. Bowling-Fresh Shoe-Deodorizing Spray (sanitizes toilets, unclogs drains, and dissolves rust).

# MR. BURNS REPL

After unwittingly sponsoring The Pin Pals registration fee due to an ether-induced hallucination, Mr. Burns decides to join the team in order to experience the fun of "reveling in the humiliation of a vanquished foe." His woeful performance endangers the team, who lose to The Stereotypes, but he finally manages to knock down two pins pulling out a miraculous win over The Holy Rollers in the finals.

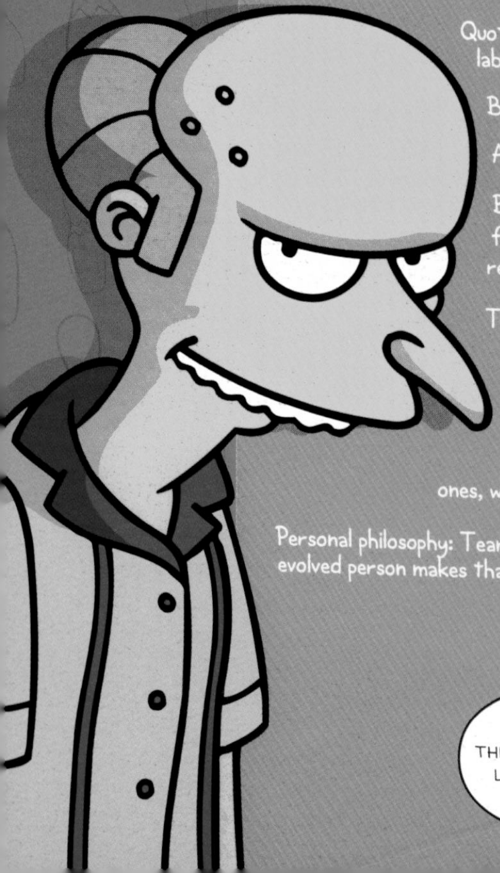

Quote: "Look at those pins topple! Just like tear-gassed labor organizers!"

Bowls: With both hands, between his legs.

Approach: Weak-kneed and seemingly endless.

Burns' Pin Pals chant: "Make way, make way for Charles Montgomery Burns!/ He paid our registration. / That's why he gets a turn!"

The Stereotypes Bowling Team: Chef Luigi, Cletus, the Slack-jawed Yokel, Groundskeeper Willie, and Captain McCallister.

Physical infirmities: Old gimpy knee gone akimbo, leprosy, every disease known to man and some new ones, which all balance each other out.

Personal philosophy: Teamwork only takes you so far. Then the truly evolved person makes that extra grab for personal glory.

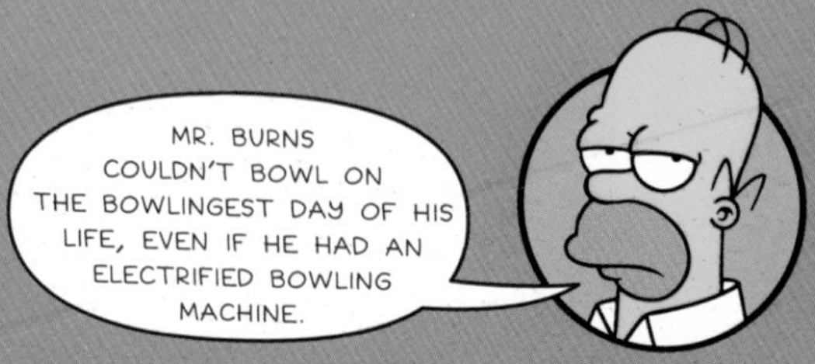
MR. BURNS COULDN'T BOWL ON THE BOWLINGEST DAY OF HIS LIFE, EVEN IF HE HAD AN ELECTRIFIED BOWLING MACHINE.

Homer begs Moe to go bowling with him so he won't have to go home to the family. As a Pin Pal, Moe bowls the final frame eliminating the DMV Regulation Kings. With The Pin Pals success, Moe is happy to be supportive of his teammates, cheering them on rather than criticizing their failures. However, when Mr. Burns joins the team, Moe attacks him with a crowbar, Tonya Harding-style, to prevent his ruining their chance at the League Championship.

Quote: "Call this an unfair generalization if you must, but old people are no good at everything."

Bowls: Right-handed.

Approach: Menacing.

Moe's Pin Pals Chant: "Go, Moe! Go, Moe! Don't make Homer shout out 'D'oh!' "

Sentimental side: Gets all choked up when given his bowling shirt, cries when he reads "My Friend Flicka" to sick kids in the hospital.

Insecurity: Doesn't think he's worth as much as fancy store-bought dirt. Regular dirt, maybe.

His attraction: An insecure, sweaty charm.

The DMV Regulation Kings Bowling Team: Patty and Selma Bouvier and their two young swains.

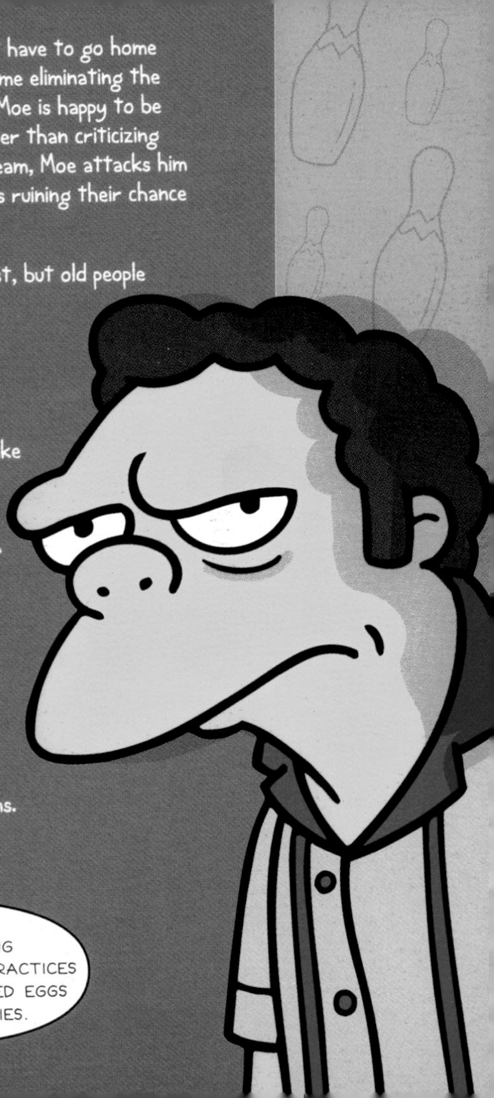

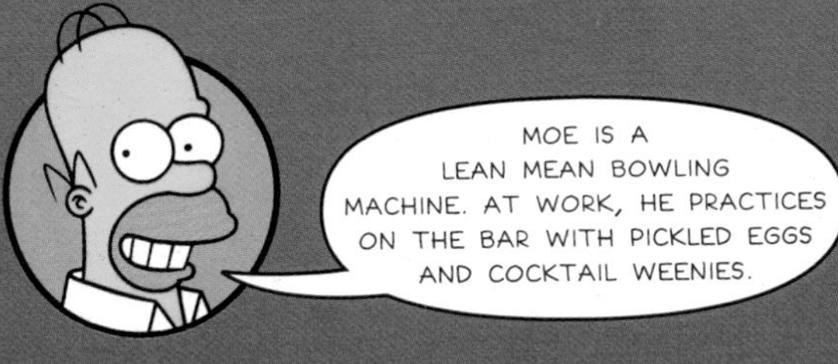
MOE IS A LEAN MEAN BOWLING MACHINE. AT WORK, HE PRACTICES ON THE BAR WITH PICKLED EGGS AND COCKTAIL WEENIES.

# APU NAHASAPEEMAPETILON MEMBER OF THE PIN PALS

Apu's initial fears that the savagery of the lanes would be too much for his fragile self-esteem are overcome by The Pin Pals camaraderie. His final strike puts pressure on The Springfield Police Framers, who forfeit, moving The Pin Pals into second place in the league standings. Despite being begged to join The Stereotypes Bowling Team, Apu sticks with The Pin Pals and experiences the thrill of winning the League Championship.

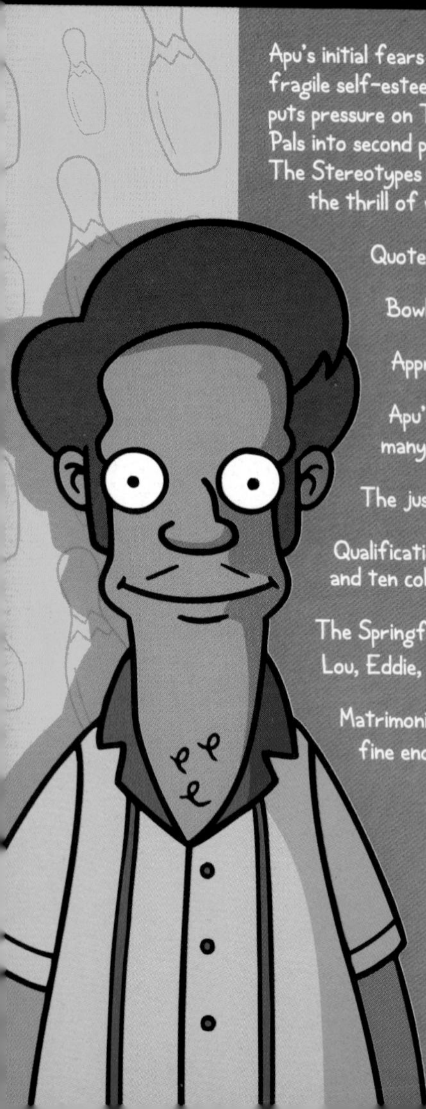

Quote: "Terrible the power of Apu, and mighty his bowling arm!"

Bowls: Right-handed.

Approach: Convoluted, but effective.

Apu's Pin Pals chant: "Apu! Apu! / Nahasapeemapetilon! / The many arms of Vishnu / Will knock those bowling pins all down!"

The just deserts of good bowling: Free gelato.

Qualifications: Played a similar game in India with a mongoose and ten cobras.

The Springfield Police Framers Bowling Team: Chief Wiggum, Lou, Eddie, and Snake (in shackles).

Matrimonial potential: Deems his Pin Pals bowling shirt a garment fine enough to be married in.

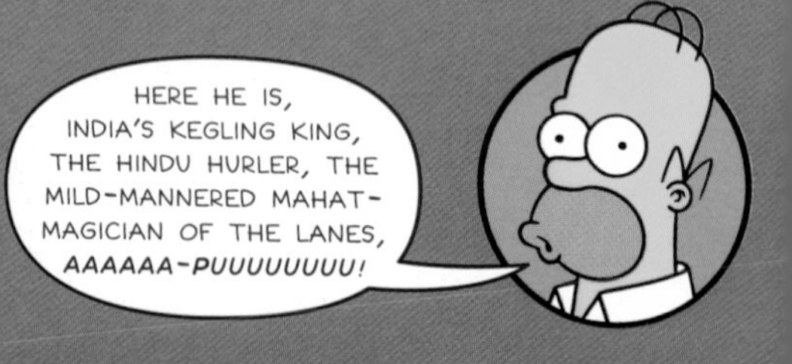
HERE HE IS, INDIA'S KEGLING KING, THE HINDU HURLER, THE MILD-MANNERED MAHAT-MAGICIAN OF THE LANES, *AAAAAA-PUUUUUUUU!*

The last member to join and the first to be replaced, Otto bowls the pivotal frame in The Pin Pals first victory, picking up a 7-10 split. The vanquished team, The Channel 6 Wastelanders, leaves in disgust. The Pin Pals celebratory beer-spraying quickly ends upon discovering the beers cost $5 each. Otto promptly wrings the beer from his hair back into the bottle and returns it.

Quote: "Whoa. Pressure's on. Don't choke, don't choke... D'oh! I choked."

Bowls: Right-handed.

Approach: Slouchy.

Otto's Pin Pals chant: "You can do it, Otto, / You can do it, Otto. / Help each other out—that'll be our motto!"

The Channel 6 Wastelanders: Kent Brockman, Arnie Pie, Krusty the Clown, and Bumblebee Man, whose shirt is embroidered with the name "Pedro."

Real reason he's at the Bowl-A-Rama: To win a Lobster Harmonica from a game of chance.

Temporary domicile: Once lived in Homer's garage.

Otto's nickname for Homer: Pop 'N' Fresh.

THAT LONG-HAIRED FREAK REALLY KNOWS HOW TO ROLL... AND BOWL.

The Holy Rollers are the most successful and most feared bowling team in Springfield. While individually their bowling skills are without peer, some suspect their success may also be due, in part, to intervention from outside forces. Their years of domination in league play have enabled The Holy Rollers to perfect the difficult art of the four-person high-five.

Celebratory Quote: "Hallelujah!"

Membership: Maude and Ned Flanders, Helen and the Rev. Timothy Lovejoy.

Bowl: Right-handed.

Approach: Doctrinaire.

Dressed for success: Monks robes with cowls, tied with a simple length of cord, matching bowling shirts underneath.

Mysterious phenomenon: Always bathed in a radiant light, sometimes accompanied by a majestic musical chord.

Moe's considered judgment: "They think they're so high and mighty, just cause they never got caught driving without pants."

Rejected team names:
The Holy Ten-Pinity,
The Ten Frame-mandments,
and Keglers for Christ.

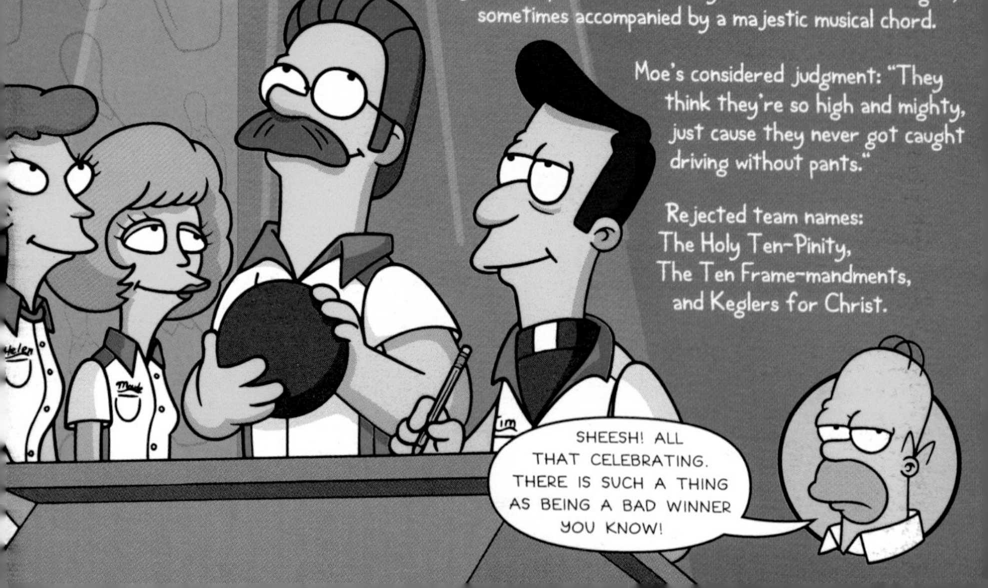
SHEESH! ALL THAT CELEBRATING. THERE IS SUCH A THING AS BEING A BAD WINNER YOU KNOW!

# JACQUES LADIES' MAN AND PROFESSIONAL BOWLING INSTRUCTOR

World weary, suave, and madly impetuous in a vaguely calculated way, Jacques is everything Homer is not. Marge finds him attentive, thoughtful, and passionately devoted to the arts of brunch, bowling, and dancing. When it comes to romance and lonely women, this Kegling Casanova usually bowls them over.

Quote: "My mind says 'stop,' but my heart and my hips cry 'proceed.'"

Garb: Turtleneck sweater.

Accent: Vaguely European, perhaps even...French.

Fingers: Slender, tapered.

Bowling team: The Home Wreckers, along with Princess Kashmir, Lurleen Lumpkin, and Mindy Simmons.

The First Lesson: "You must get to know your lane. Feel the slickness. Feel the satiny finish. Caress it. Experience it."

Instructional rate: $40 per hour; $25 per hour for the extremely fairer sex.

Residence: The Fiesta Terrace Apartments for Single Living.

Medicine cabinet: Filled with a wide assortment of enticing colognes.

Musical preference: Smooth jazz as exemplified by The Steve Sax Trio.

Pets: A white standard poodle.

Dietary advice: "Laugh! Laugh out loud! You'll lose weight."

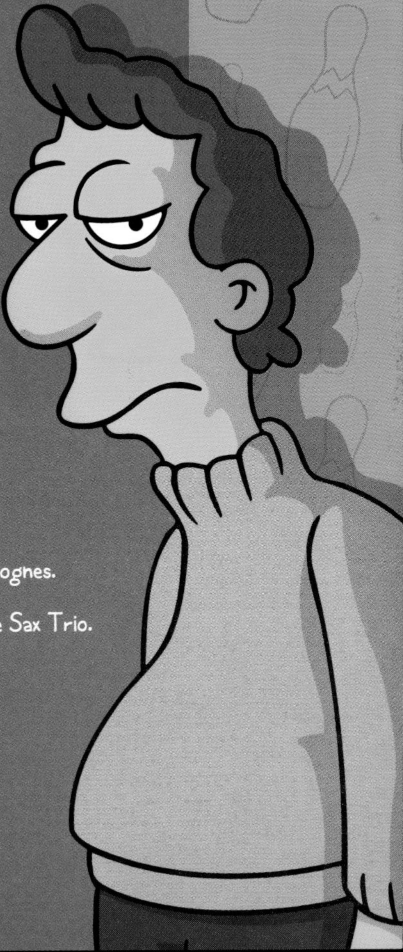

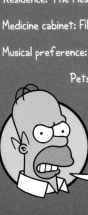

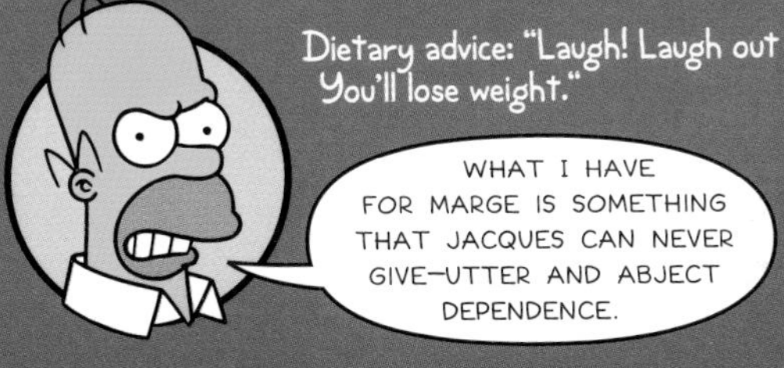
WHAT I HAVE FOR MARGE IS SOMETHING THAT JACQUES CAN NEVER GIVE—UTTER AND ABJECT DEPENDENCE.

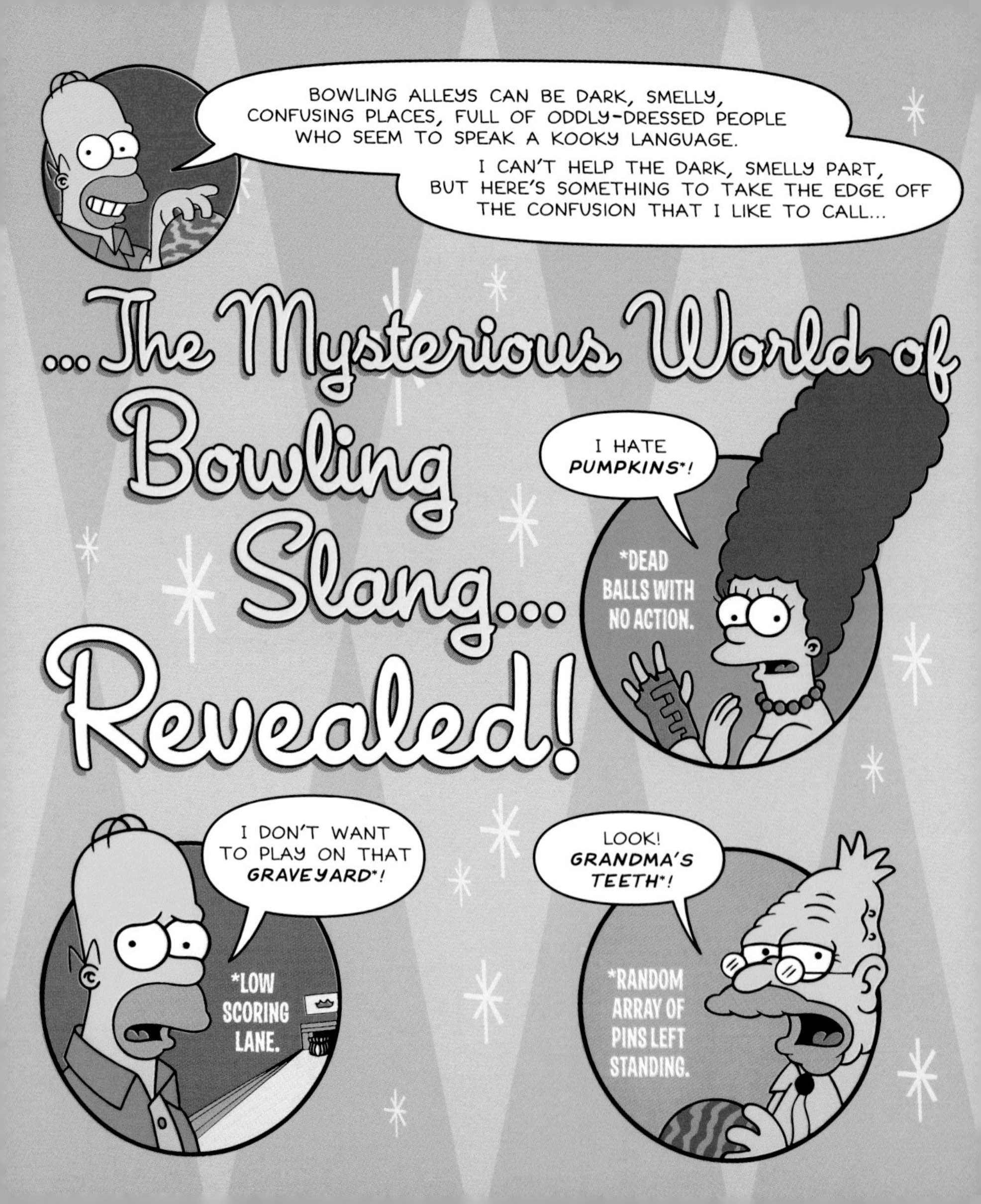
BOWLING ALLEYS CAN BE DARK, SMELLY, CONFUSING PLACES, FULL OF ODDLY-DRESSED PEOPLE WHO SEEM TO SPEAK A KOOKY LANGUAGE.
I CAN'T HELP THE DARK, SMELLY PART, BUT HERE'S SOMETHING TO TAKE THE EDGE OFF THE CONFUSION THAT I LIKE TO CALL...
...The Mysterious World of Bowling Slang... Revealed!
I HATE PUMPKINS*!
*DEAD BALLS WITH NO ACTION.
I DON'T WANT TO PLAY ON THAT GRAVEYARD*!
*LOW SCORING LANE.
LOOK! GRANDMA'S TEETH*!
*RANDOM ARRAY OF PINS LEFT STANDING.

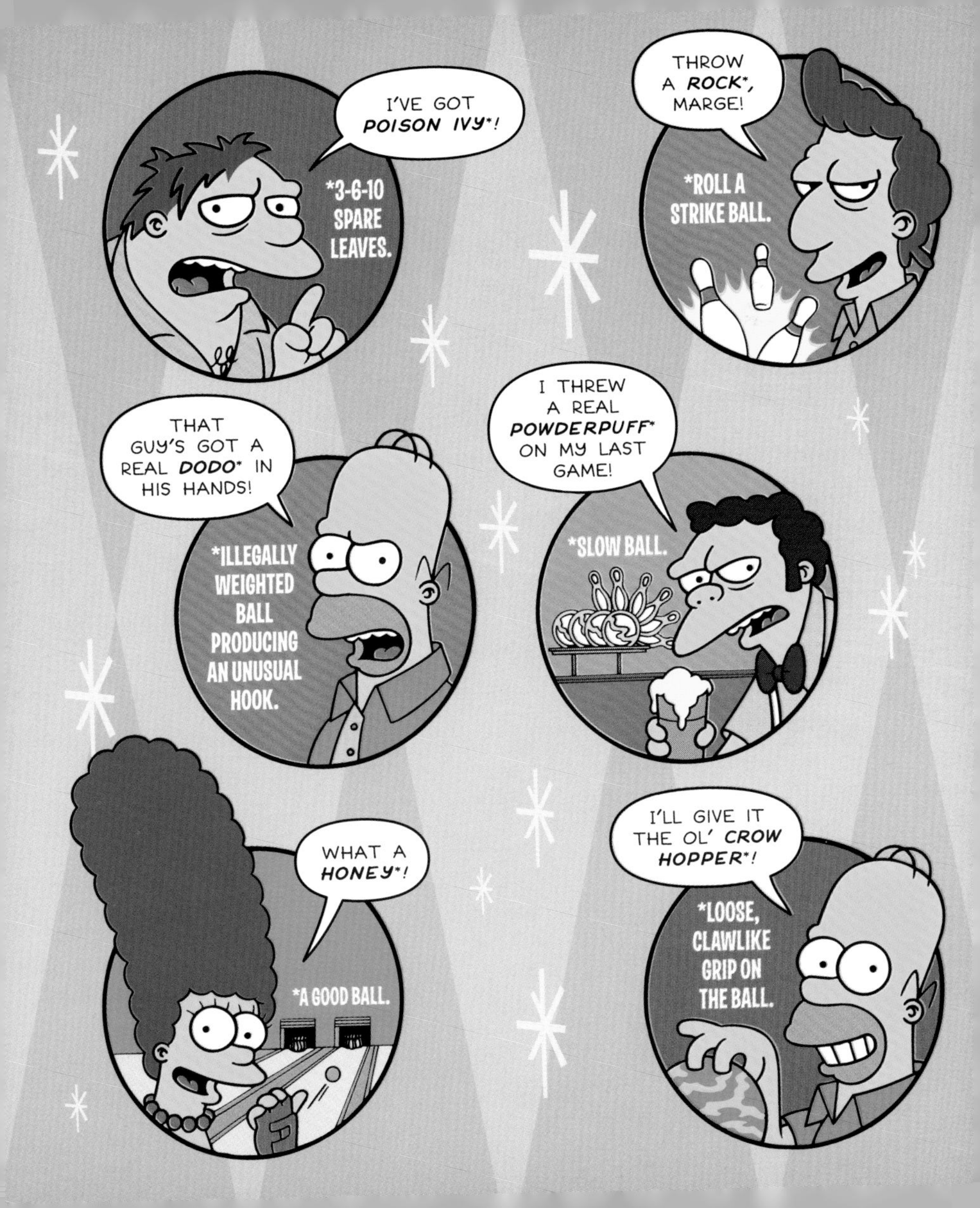
I'VE GOT POISON IVY*!
*3-6-10 SPARE LEAVES.
THROW A ROCK*, MARGE!
*ROLL A STRIKE BALL.
THAT GUY'S GOT A REAL DODO* IN HIS HANDS!
*ILLEGALLY WEIGHTED BALL PRODUCING AN UNUSUAL HOOK.
I THREW A REAL POWDERPUFF* ON MY LAST GAME!
*SLOW BALL.
WHAT A HONEY*!
*A GOOD BALL.
I'LL GIVE IT THE OL' CROW HOPPER*!
*LOOSE, CLAWLIKE GRIP ON THE BALL.

# PRESENTING
# Homer
## THE CAR BUILT FOR HOMER

1. BOWLING TROPHY HOOD ORNAMENT
2. DELUXE SUPERCHARGED V8 ENGINE
3. HORN THAT PLAYS "LA CUCARACHA"
4. FLUORESCENT ANTENNA BALL TO HELP FIND CAR IN PARKING LOT
5. SOUNDPROOF BUBBLE DOME FOR THE KIDS (W/ OPTIONAL RESTRAINTS & MUZZLES)
6. SPOILER
7. TAIL FINS
8. EXTRA-NOISY YEAR-ROUND SNOW TIRES
9. EXTREMELY LARGE BEVERAGE HOLDER TO ACCOMMODATE SUPER SLAKERS FROM KWIK-E-MART
10. TRUCK-SIZED SIDE VIEW MIRROR
11. DRIVER-SIDE STEPLADDER
12. BART-VIEW MIRROR
13. FURRY STEERING WHEEL COVER
14. DELUXE CHROME NAME PLATE
15. HIGH BEAM / LOW BEAM / LOWER BEAM HEADLIGHTS
16. FAUX ROLLS-ROYCE GRILL

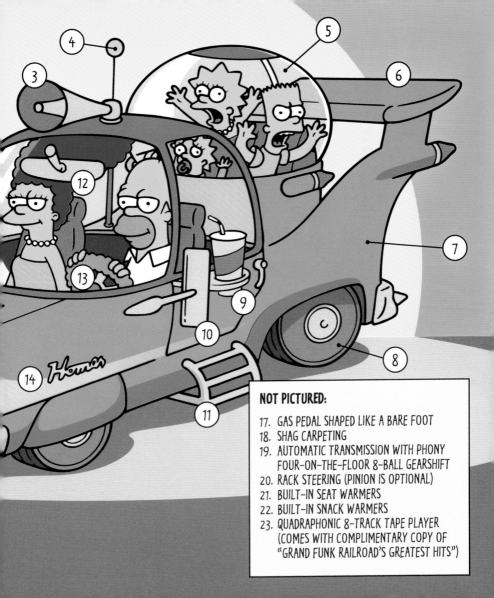

**NOT PICTURED:**

17. GAS PEDAL SHAPED LIKE A BARE FOOT
18. SHAG CARPETING
19. AUTOMATIC TRANSMISSION WITH PHONY FOUR-ON-THE-FLOOR 8-BALL GEARSHIFT
20. RACK STEERING (PINION IS OPTIONAL)
21. BUILT-IN SEAT WARMERS
22. BUILT-IN SNACK WARMERS
23. QUADRAPHONIC 8-TRACK TAPE PLAYER (COMES WITH COMPLIMENTARY COPY OF "GRAND FUNK RAILROAD'S GREATEST HITS")

# LITTLE KNOWN FACT:

Homer's lifelong dreams include: becoming a monorail conductor, running out onto a baseball field during a game, managing a beautiful country western singer, eating the world's biggest hoagie, becoming a blackjack dealer, appearing on "The Gong Show," owning the Dallas Cowboys, living in the wilderness while keeping a journal of his thoughts, working in a bowling alley, and bowling a perfect game. He has accomplished all of these goals except for living in the wilderness while keeping a journal of his thoughts and owning the Dallas Cowboys. He did, however, own the Denver Broncos.

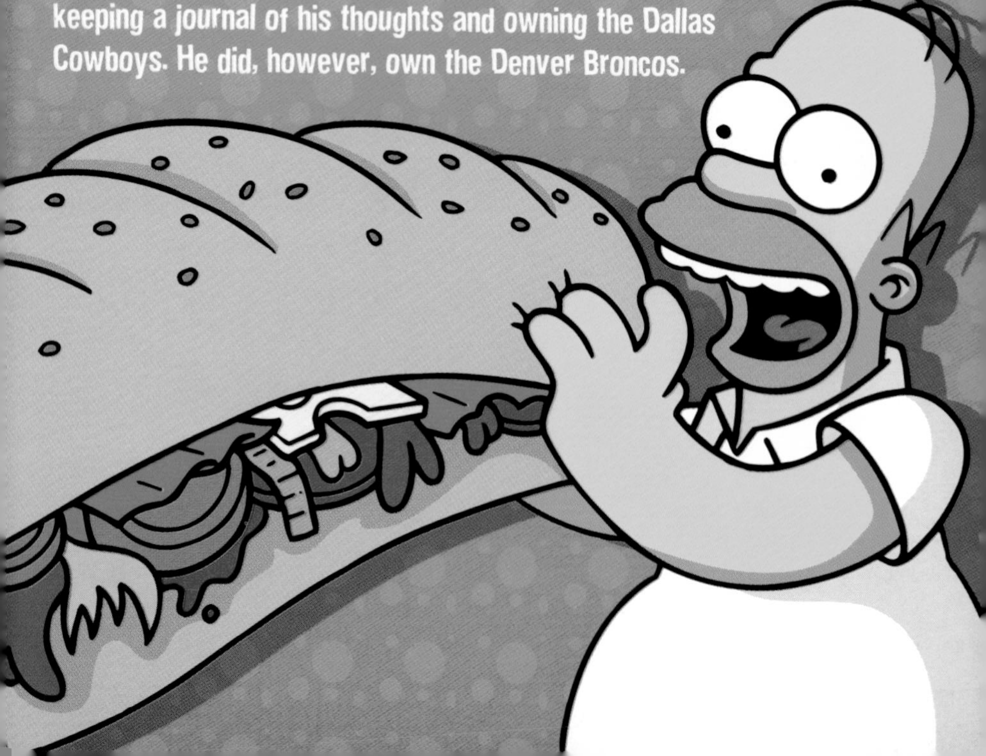

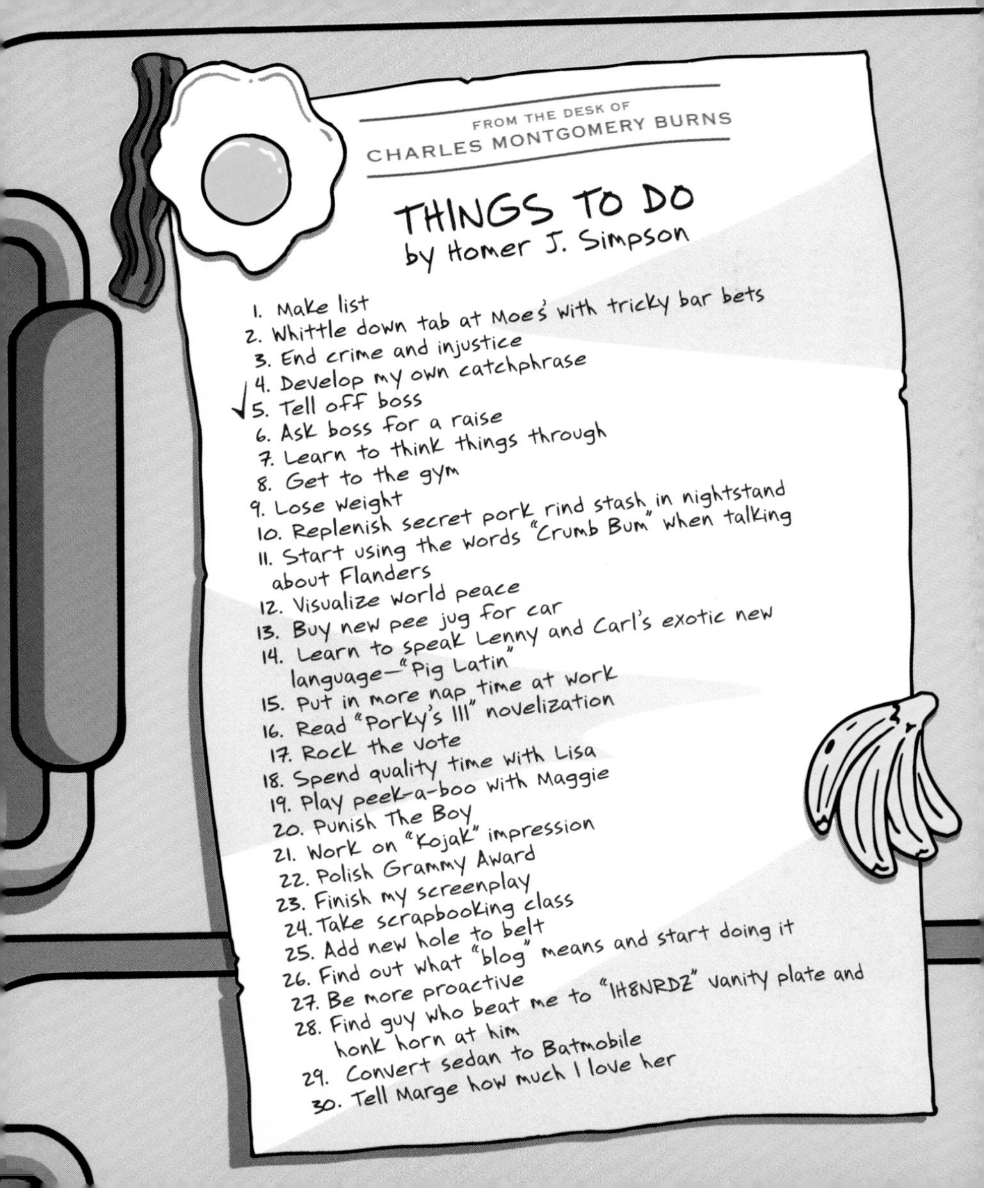
FROM THE DESK OF
CHARLES MONTGOMERY BURNS
THINGS TO DO
by Homer J. Simpson
1. Make list
2. Whittle down tab at Moe's with tricky bar bets
3. End crime and injustice
4. Develop my own catchphrase
✓5. Tell off boss
6. Ask boss for a raise
7. Learn to think things through
8. Get to the gym
9. Lose weight
10. Replenish secret pork rind stash in nightstand
11. Start using the words "Crumb Bum" when talking about Flanders
12. Visualize world peace
13. Buy new pee jug for car
14. Learn to speak Lenny and Carl's exotic new language—"Pig Latin"
15. Put in more nap time at work
16. Read "Porky's III" novelization
17. Rock the vote
18. Spend quality time with Lisa
19. Play peek-a-boo with Maggie
20. Punish The Boy
21. Work on "Kojak" impression
22. Polish Grammy Award
23. Finish my screenplay
24. Take scrapbooking class
25. Add new hole to belt
26. Find out what "blog" means and start doing it
27. Be more proactive
28. Find guy who beat me to "IH8NRDZ" vanity plate and honk horn at him
29. Convert sedan to Batmobile
30. Tell Marge how much I love her

*THE SIMPSONS' ICEBOX. CHILLY CONVEYOR OF COMFORT FOOD, STURDY SENTRY OF STAPLES, AND YET, SO MUCH MORE! REVEALED HERE, FOR THE FIRST TIME...*

# ...The Mysteries of Homer's Fridge!

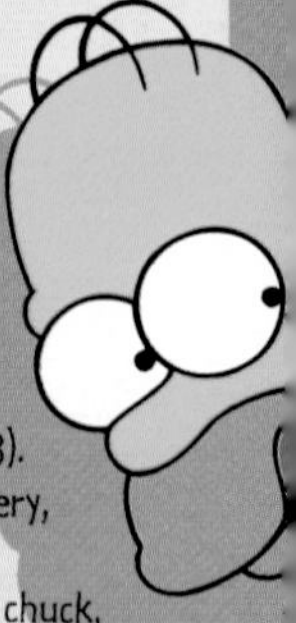

1. Mr. Meatball Meatball Mix. (Just add onions.)
2. Air Biscuit Brand Aromatic Biscuit Mix.
3. Swampy Joe's Cajun Jambalaya! ("You'll roux the day you don't try it!")
4. Sideshow Mel's Milk 'N' Cookies in a Carton.
5. Mustetchupaise "Mustard, Ketchup and Mayonnaise – All in One Bottle! Now with Relish!"
6. Mustard (stolen from Springfield Stadium).
7. Ketchup (stolen from Krustyburger).
8. Salad Dressing (stolen from Paul Newman).
9. Spring water (from concentrate).
10. Maggie's bottles labeled "Homer! Do not drink!"
11. Farmer Krusty's Bacon-flavored Butter.
12. Dennis Franz's COP TARTS. "The Breakfast that Takes Down Hunger!" —"NYPD Blueberry" Flavor.
13. 14 real eggs and 1 fake one with a house key inside.
14. Five Han Solo action figures, frozen in blocks of ice since 1980.
15. Itchy & Scratchy "Guts 'N' Entrails' Dinner" (Spaghetti & Meatballs).
16. Three frozen, ready-to-explode cans of Buzz Cola.
17. Homer's Secret Rainy Day fund.
18. Krustcicles.
19. Gabbopops (circa 1996).
20. Cookie Jar #4. Currently contains 3/4ths of a Fudge Stripe cookie and a single Oreo top.
21. Cookbooks, including: "Fluffer Nutters and Other Peanut Butter/Marshmallow Spread Recipes," "Slaw Anything," "Toledo Cookin'!," "The Gravy Bible,"and "How to Make Vegetables Taste Like Meat."
22. Two sixteen-cube capacity ice trays (empty).
23. Homer's Cold Cap (An old army helmet Homer keeps in the freezer for sweltering days).
24. A gallon freezer bag of Chief Wiggum's chili (for use in vision quests).
25. Inflatable raft.
26. Colonel Krusty's Fried Chicken Parts Dinner with Mystery Cobbler.
27. Brigadier General Krusty's Salisbury Steak Dinner with Mystery Pudding.
28. Raj Krusty's Paneer Dinner with Mystery Biryani.
29. Marge's Secret Rainy Day Fund: $507 in a Greenman's Broccoli Florets box.
30. Soygurt.
31. Box of frozen Reggie! bars (circa 1983).
32. Ally McMeal: Frozen Carrot Sticks, Celery, and Water (circa 1997).
33. Ralph-Abets — bite-sized chunks of chuck, shaped like letters, in a savory gray liquid.
34. Marge's Up-and-Coming Walnut Ambrosia Icebox Cake.
35. Krustofski Vineyards Bulk Red Wine (not kosher).
36. MAYOMANIA!
37. "Real Yolks " Brand Egg Yolk Substitute Alternative.
38. Bagel-flavored Cream Cheese.
39. High-gloss, quick-drying chocolate syrup.
40. Cloudy D (Non-alcoholic Duff juice drink for kids).
41. Homer's Mystery Punch (1 part Hawaiian Punch 1 part flat beer).
42. Duff Chai in biodegradable spun soy bottles. (Bought by mistake.)
43. Duff Hard Lemonade.
44. Duff Non-Alcoholic-But-Still-Extremely-Hard Lemonade.
45. Duff Gummy Ale.
46. Duff Sour Apple Lager.
47. Open box of Baking Soda (circa 1992).
48. Marge's Obscure Artichoke Lasagna.
49. Marge's Famous Gelatin Fish Loaf.
50. Paint thinner (for some reason).
51. Rarely opened mystery produce bin.

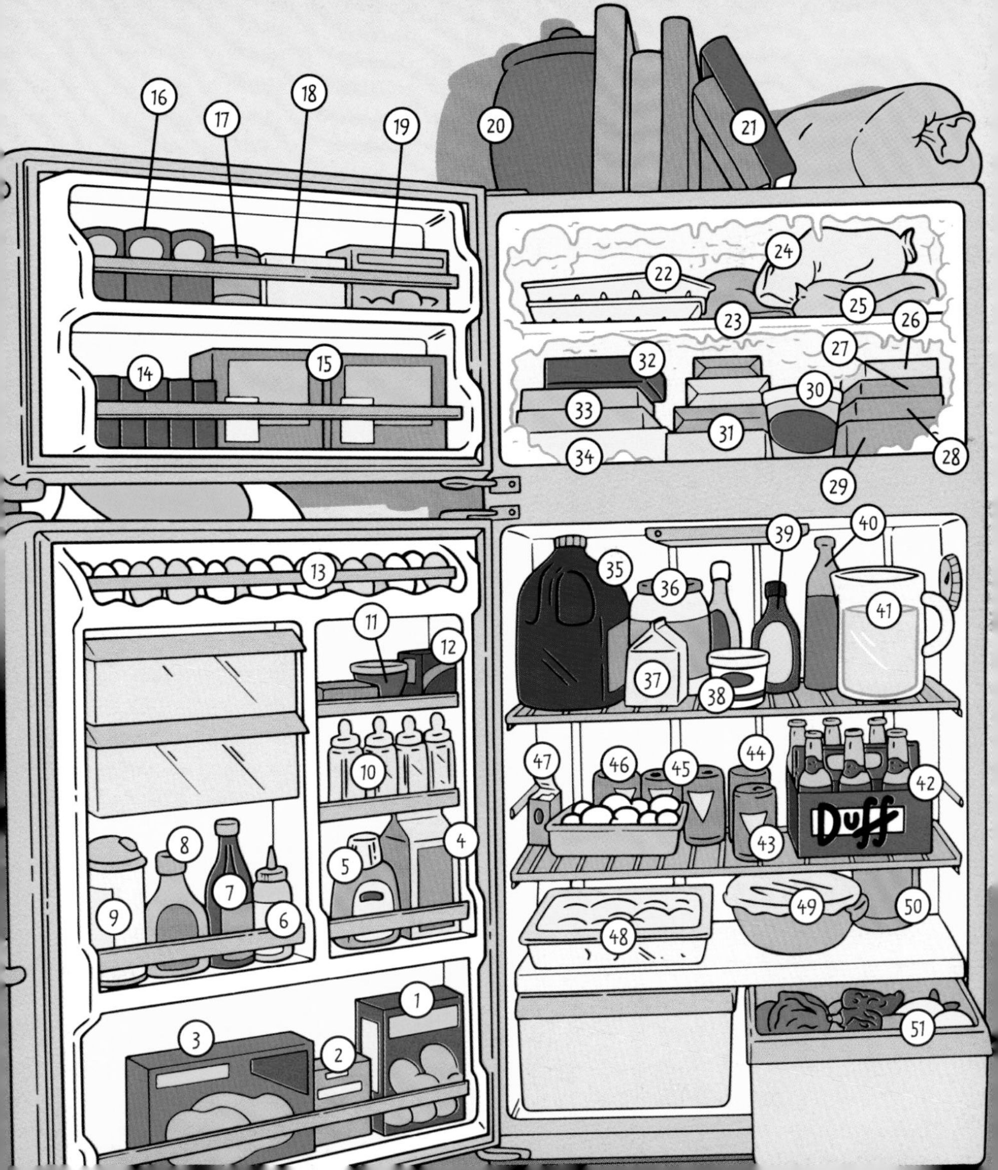
16
17
18
19
20
21
14
15
22
23
24
25
26
27
28
29
30
31
32
33
34
13
35
36
37
38
39
40
41
11
12
10
47
46
45
44
43
42
Duff
8
7
9
6
5
4
48
49
50
51
1
2
3

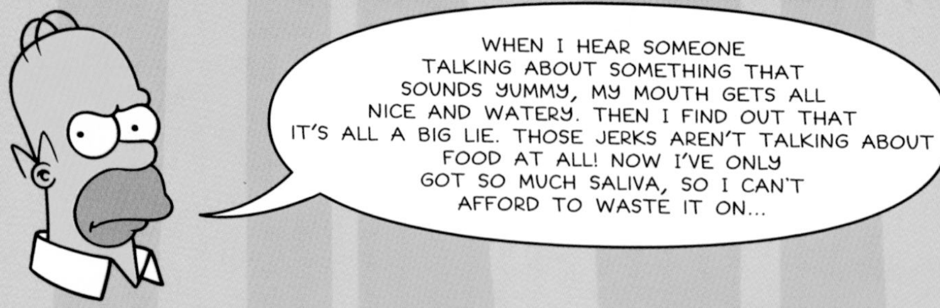
WHEN I HEAR SOMEONE TALKING ABOUT SOMETHING THAT SOUNDS YUMMY, MY MOUTH GETS ALL NICE AND WATERY. THEN I FIND OUT THAT IT'S ALL A BIG LIE. THOSE JERKS AREN'T TALKING ABOUT FOOD AT ALL! NOW I'VE ONLY GOT SO MUCH SALIVA, SO I CAN'T AFFORD TO WASTE IT ON...

# ...THINGS THAT SOUND LIKE FOOD, BUT AREN'T!

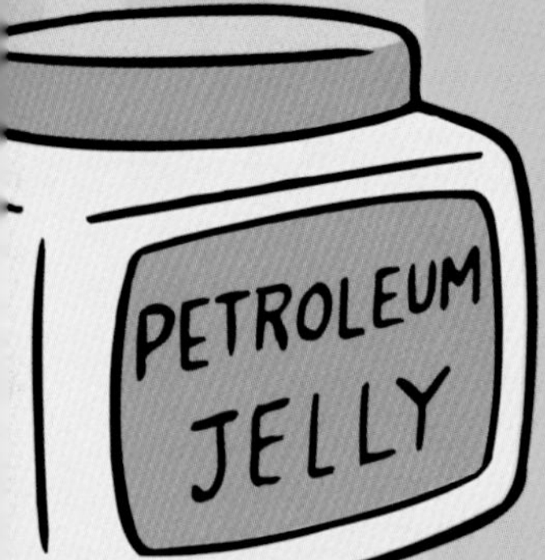
PETROLEUM JELLY

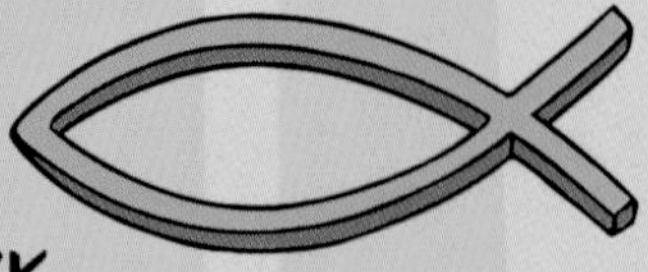

*ROAD APPLES*

*JESUS FISH*

*VANILLA ICE*

*PETROLEUM JELLY*

*URINAL CAKES*

*COW PIE*

*THE SPICE GIRLS*

*CONDOLEEZZA RICE*

*HAMBURG, GERMANY*

*WING NUTS*

*SIX PACK ABS*

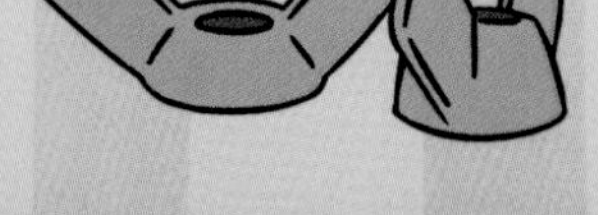

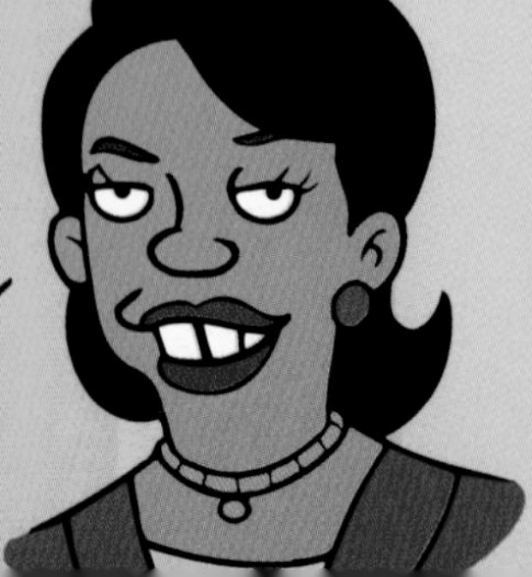

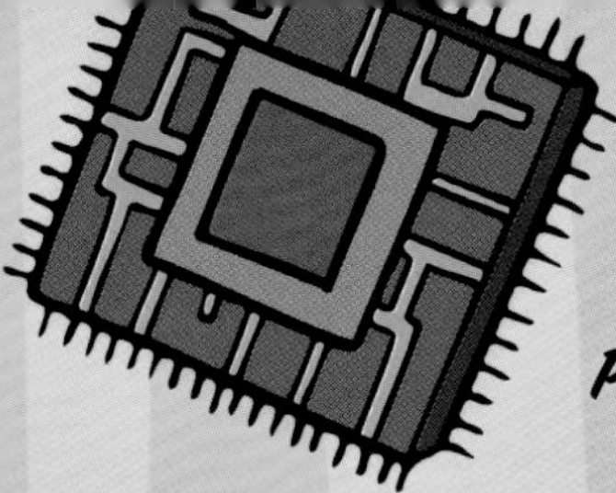

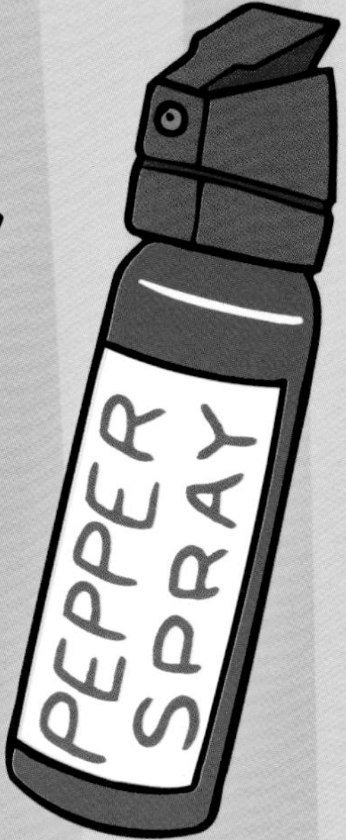
PEPPER
SPRAY

TOE JAM

MICROCHIPS

PORK BARREL SPENDING

DINGLEBERRIES

PEPPER SPRAY

JIVE TURKEY

THE MAYO CLINIC

DRUM STICKS

DISCO STU

L'EGGS

SALMONELLA

LUG NUTS

HEMORRHOID DONUT

HUMBLE PIE

PACKING PEANUTS

COUCH POTATOES

CORN PADS

SOUPY SALES

FRUIT CAKE

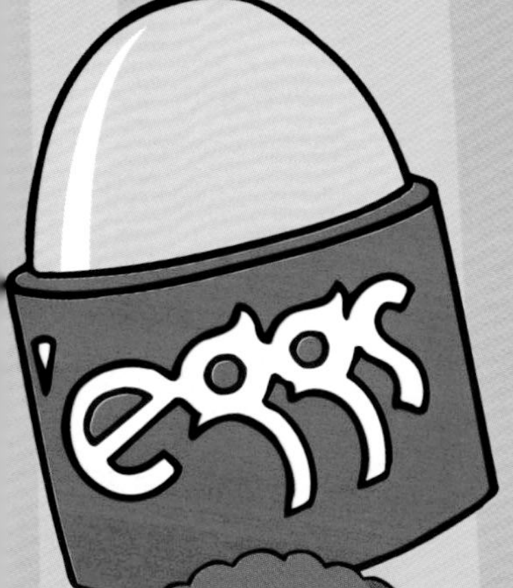

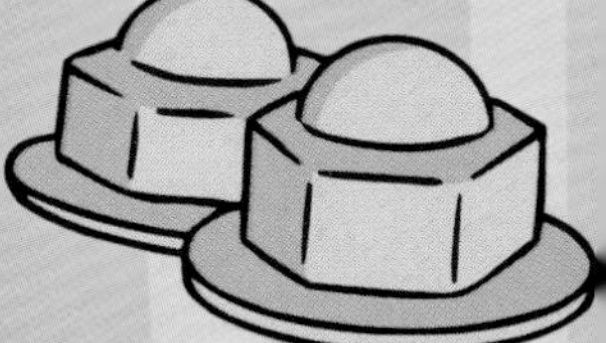

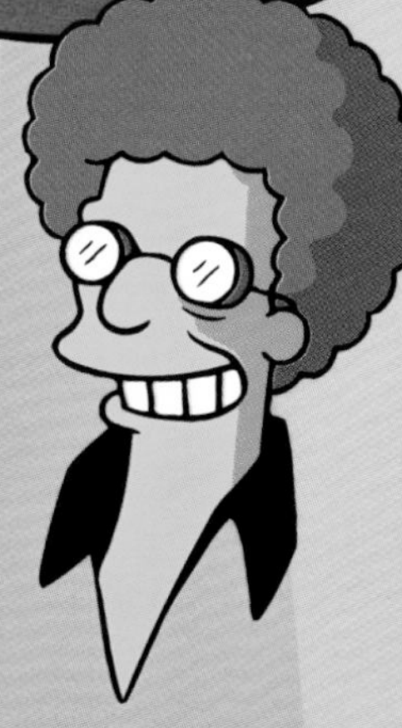

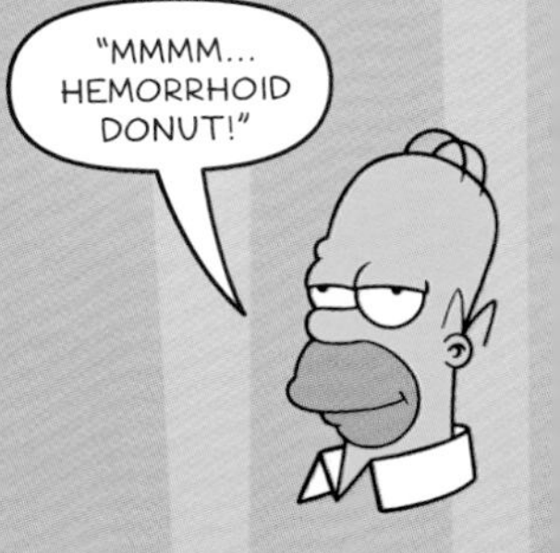
"MMMM... HEMORRHOID DONUT!"

AAH, THE UNIVERSE IS **BACK** IN BALANCE! I JUST DISCOVERED THERE ARE ALSO...

# ...THINGS THAT DON'T SOUND LIKE FOOD, BUT ARE!

LADYFINGERS

TOAD IN THE HOLE

NAPOLEONS

GRINDERS

HEROES

CAPERS

MUSELIX

DAGWOODS

LOX

HASH

PIGS IN A BLANKET

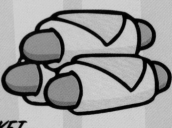

PO' BOYS

SCRAPPLE

SLOPPY JOES

COOL WHIP

BAKED ALASKA

FLAPJACKS

HUSH PUPPIES

JERKY

GRITS

ELEPHANT EARS

SAND DABS

ROLL MOPS

VEGEMITE

HOT DOGS

TOFU

ZWIEBACK

HUMMUS

PU PU PLATTER

BROWN BETTY

"MMMM...
SCRAPPLE!"

# THE MANY MOODS OF

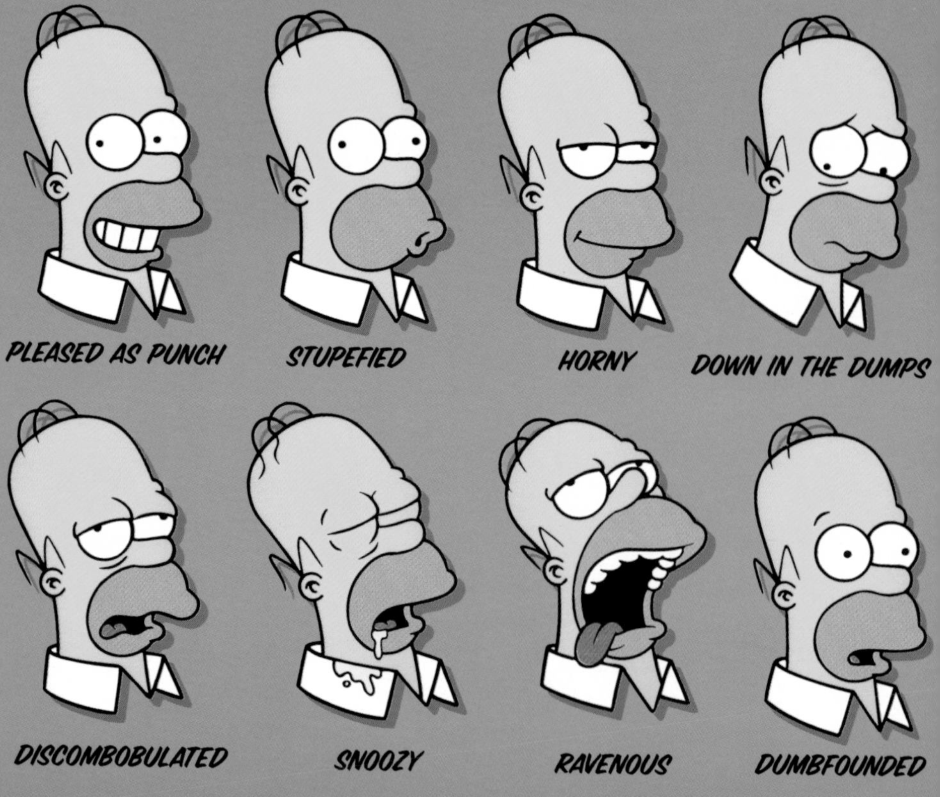

PLEASED AS PUNCH
STUPEFIED
HORNY
DOWN IN THE DUMPS
DISCOMBOBULATED
SNOOZY
RAVENOUS
DUMBFOUNDED

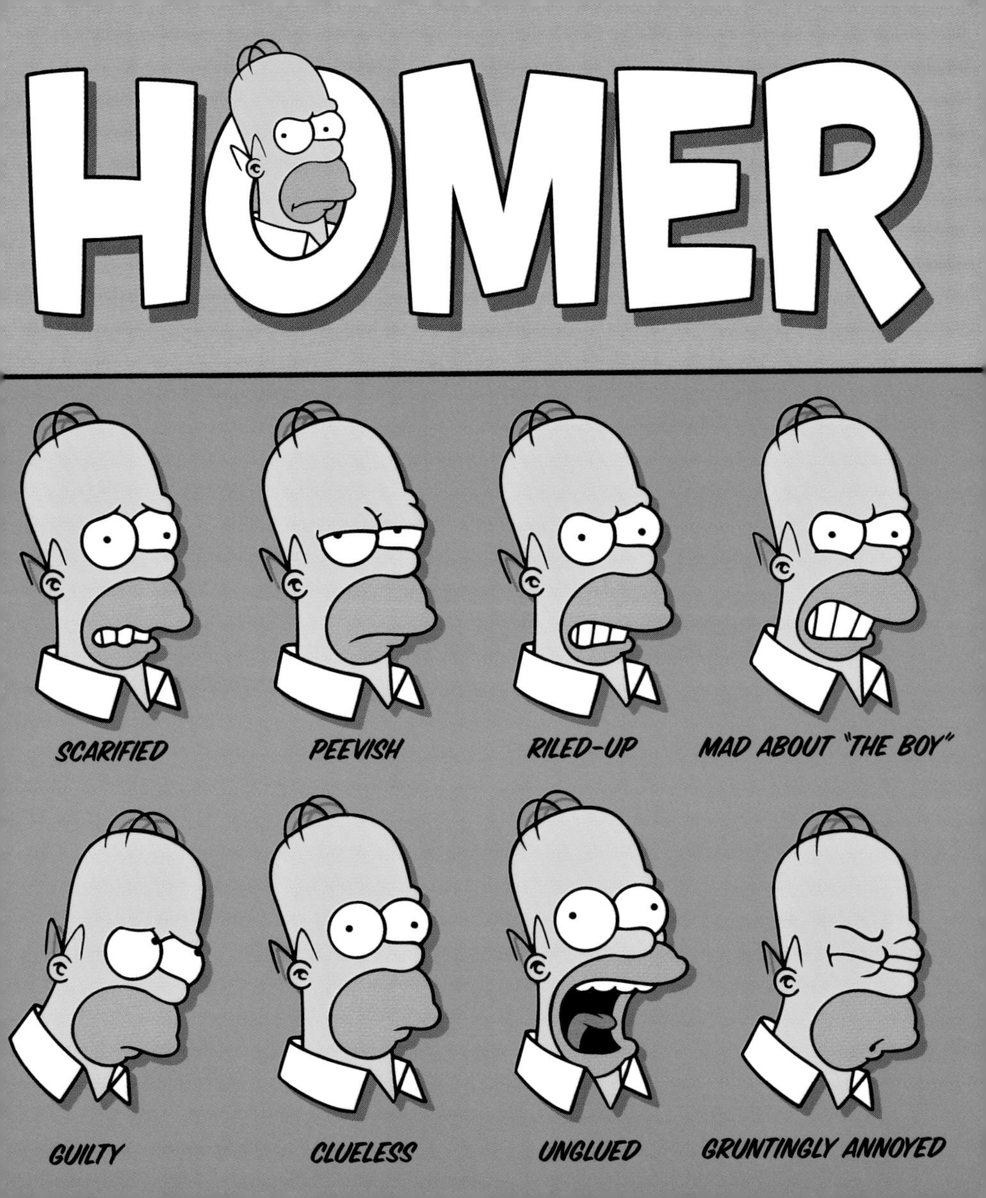
HOMER
SCARIFIED
PEEVISH
RILED-UP
MAD ABOUT "THE BOY"
GUILTY
CLUELESS
UNGLUED
GRUNTINGLY ANNOYED

# HOMER'S HAUNTS

# the KWIK-E-MART

1. Tourist film camera stand.
2. Impulse items (naked lady ink pens, Kap'n Krusty's Chawin' Baccy, "Kwik-E-Mart's Most Wanted Check Bouncers" playing cards).
3. Breakfast options [fresh day-old donuts at week-old prices (fancies extra), donut holes, muffin stumps (tops sold separately), curry crullers, reclaimed sprinkles].
4. Freezer Case (with Frostillicus).
5. Sage advice.
6. Deep-fried pickles.
7. Plastic jar of desiccated meat-like jerky chew.
8. Bombay surprise (shotgun under counter).
9. Charity donation bucket (Krusty the Clown's Marathon for Motion Sickness).
10. Kwik-E-Mart heart and soul.
11. Squishee machine. (New Chutney Flavor!)
12. Magazine Racks (includes such stellar publications as: "Vicarious Living," "Bar & Stool," "Mosh Pitter," "Danger Liker," "Meddling Today," "Non-Threatening Boys," "Bear Baiter Magazine," "Jugs & Ammo").
13. Duff Beer-amid.
14. Great White Hunter video game.
15. Heat-lamp dogs.
16. Never-washed condiment tray.
17. Closed-circuit store monitor.
18. Fully-cooked caffeinated sludge.
19. Non-dairy powdered cream-like substitute in difficult-to-open packages.
20. Unseen in janitor closet: shrine to Ganesha.

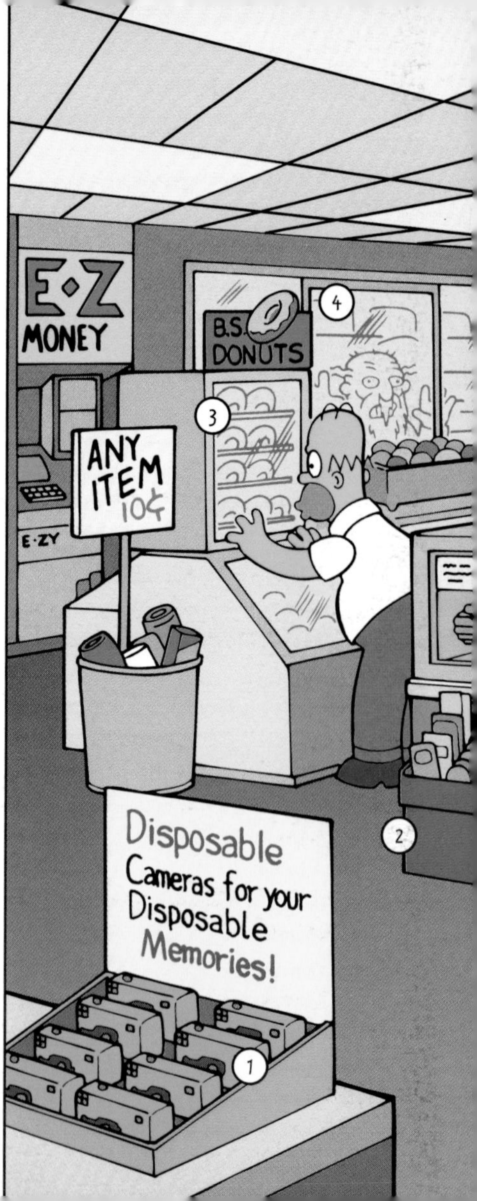

E·Z MONEY
E·ZY
B.S. DONUTS
ANY ITEM 10¢
Disposable Cameras for your Disposable Memories!
1
2
3
4

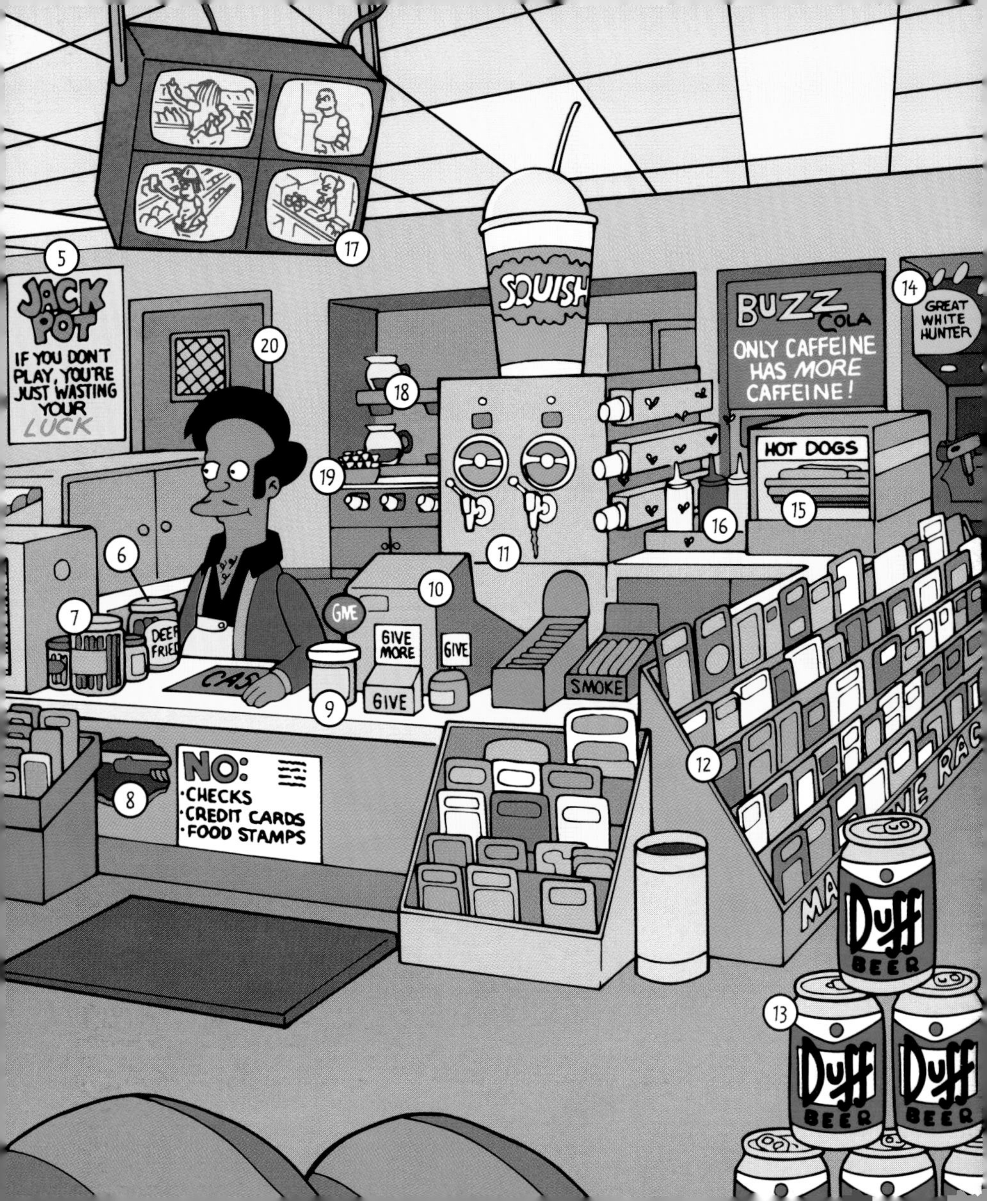
5
JACK POT
IF YOU DON'T PLAY, YOU'RE JUST WASTING YOUR LUCK
17
20
SQUISH
BUZZ COLA
ONLY CAFFEINE HAS MORE CAFFEINE!
14
GREAT WHITE HUNTER
18
19
HOT DOGS
15
16
11
6
7
10
GIVE
GIVE MORE
GIVE
GIVE
SMOKE
9
8
NO:
·CHECKS
·CREDIT CARDS
·FOOD STAMPS
12
Duff BEER
13
Duff BEER
Duff BEER

# APU NAHASAPEEMAPETILON EVER-PRESENT MANAGER AT KWIK-E-MART

Coming from India in search of The Land of Opportunity, Apu settles for Springfield and the local Kwik-E-Mart. Apu's marketing innovations include: the first use of disappearing ink in expiration dates, the Chutney Squishee, and "Frank," a dynamic new fragrance for men distilled from the run-off of heat-lamp dogs. His autobiography "From Ragas to Riches" is considered the bible of the convenience store industry.

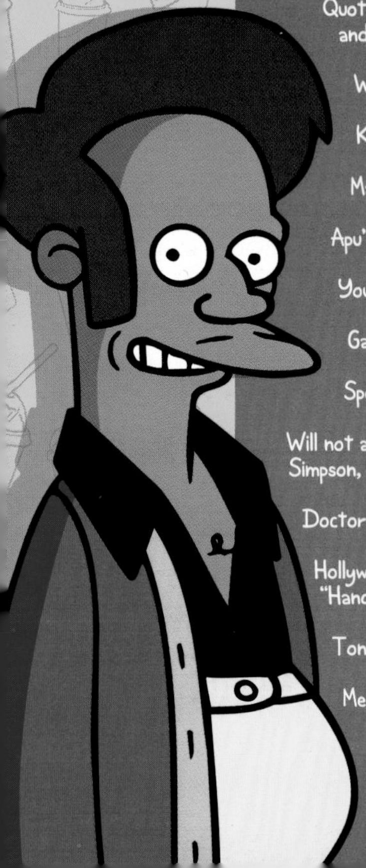

Quote: "I love this land where I have the freedom to say, and to think, and to charge whatever I want."

Wife: Manjula.

Kids: Poonam, Sashi, Pria, Uma, Anoop, Sandeep, Nabendu, and Gheet.

Manjula's dowry: Ten goats, an electric fan, and a textile factory.

Apu's favorite come-on: "You are one Mahat-mama!"

Younger brother and co-worker: Sanjay.

Garments: All polyester, all the time.

Special skills: Price-gouging, expiration date-altering, and bullet-dodging.

Will not accept checks from: Chief Wiggum, Reverend Lovejoy, Homer J. Simpson, Homer S. Simpson, H.J. Simpson, Homor Simpson, Homer J. Fong.

Doctor of Mixology: Invented the Champagne Squishee for Valentine's Day.

Hollywood dream: To have his autobiographical screenplay, "Hands Off My Jerky, Turkey" produced.

Tonsorial destination: Hairy Shearers.

Merchandising Nemesis: The nearby Gulp 'N' Blow.

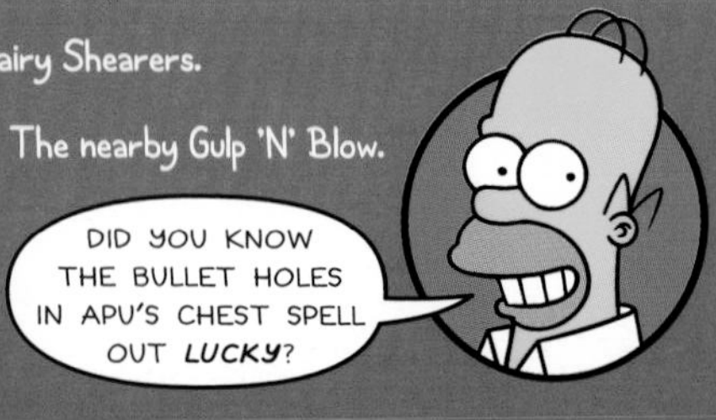
DID YOU KNOW THE BULLET HOLES IN APU'S CHEST SPELL OUT *LUCKY*?

Snake's criminal career officially begins at the age of twelve, when he appoints himself Springfield Junior High Wallet Inspector. His illustrious record includes the robbing of banks, hotels, convenience stores, lemonade stands, credit card fraud, car theft, and loitering. His numerous Kwik-E-Mart heists are widely credited for the Great Beef Jerky Shortage of 1991.

Quote: "Ho-ho! I'll be back on the street in 24 hours!"

Identifying details: Tattoo of a fanged serpent on his arm, hair worn in pompadour using "Nacho Cheez" for styling gel, large hoop earring in his ear, and ripped sleeveless denim jacket.

Pet: A boa constrictor named Snake, Jr.

Pet peeve: Drivers who slow down at red lights.

Secret shame: Dressed up as a ballerina for the game show "How Low Will You Go?"

Tools of the trade: Sawed-off shotgun, butcher knife, deck of cards, Acme Piano Wire, getaway car.

License plates: "EX CON" and "GR8 68"

His car's name: L'il Bandit.

Auto adornment: Tiny skull hanging from rearview mirror.

Turn-ons: Trashing the stage at rock concerts, the freedom and security of unmarked bills, and the smooth sensuous feel of nylon rope.

Turn-offs: Cops. Both the show, and the individuals.

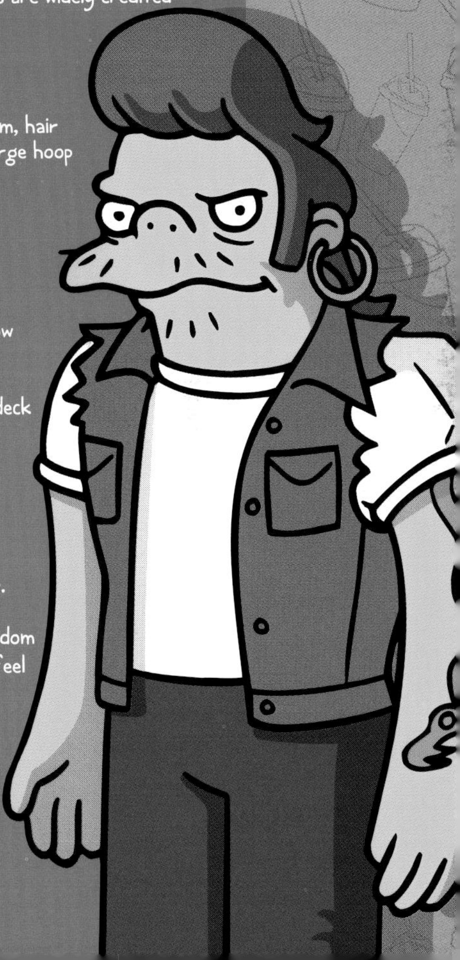

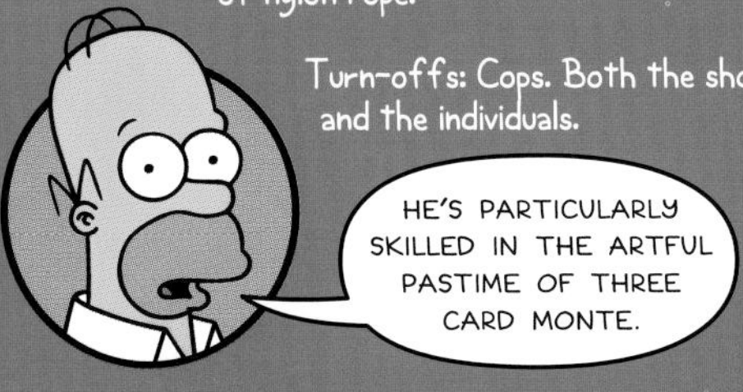
HE'S PARTICULARLY SKILLED IN THE ARTFUL PASTIME OF THREE CARD MONTE.

This incredibly popular and powerful Japanese dish detergent would sweep through the households of America like a tsunami if only unfair U.S. trade embargoes were lifted, thereby familiarizing the populace with its uncanny likeness of Homer Simpson. Until then, Homer will have to toil in anonymity, his doughy features known only to a chosen few.

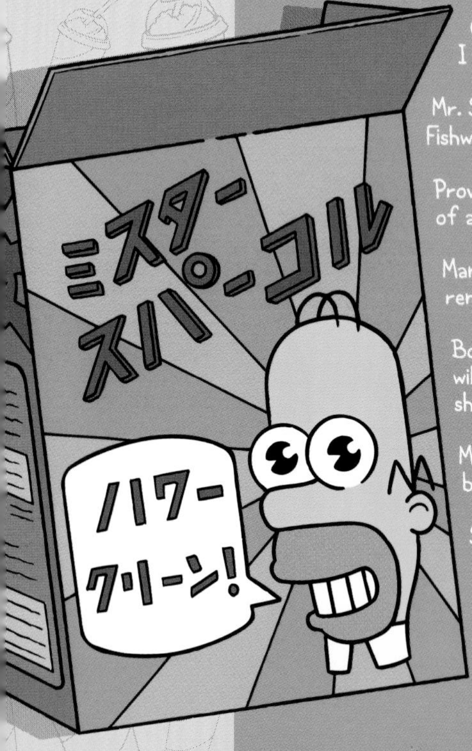
ミスター
スパーコル
ハワー
クリーン!

Quote: "I am disrespectful to dirt! Can you see that I am serious?"

Mr. Sparkle's producers: Joint venture of Matsumura Fishworks and Tamaribuchi Heavy Manufacturing Concern.

Provenance of the Mr. Sparkle logo: The happy melding of a lightbulb and a fish.

Manufactured in: Sacred Forest of Hokkaido, renowned for its countless soap factories.

Boastful self-attributions: Magnet for foodstuffs, will banish dirt to the land of wind and ghosts, can shatter two-headed cows like glass.

Musical tendencies: Plays the xylophone, befriended by a little red monkey who beats a drum.

Super ability: Can fly both through the air and underwater, possesses transformational magic dust.

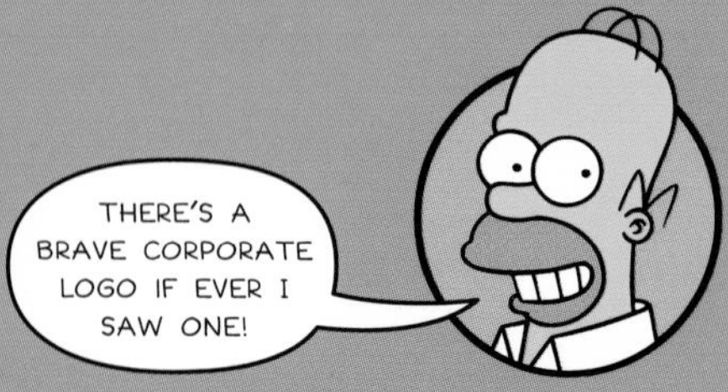
THERE'S A BRAVE CORPORATE LOGO IF EVER I SAW ONE!

# KWIK-E-MART C.E.O. TOP DOG, KWIK-E-MART CORPORATION

The ultimate arbiter of all things convenient, the Kwik-E-Mart C.E.O. fields questions both weighty and mundane from the summit of one of the most majestic peaks at the top of the world, thus avoiding all but the peskiest of questioners. A strict allotment of three questions is also imposed, limiting the litigiousness of labor lawyers, the harrying of health inspectors, and the annoyance of accountants.

Quote: "I hope this has been enlightening for you. Thank you. Come again."

Motto: "The master knows all except combination to safe."

Official title: Benevolent Enlightened President and C.E.O. of Kwik-E-Mart (and in Ohio, Stop-O-Mart)

Corporate headquarters: World's first convenience store, high atop a mountain in India.

Garb: Long-flowing white robes.

Identifying features: Long-flowing white hair, beatific grin.

Voice: Mellifluous, soothing yet firm.

Posture: Full Lotus position.

Favorite beverage:
The Sublime Squishee.

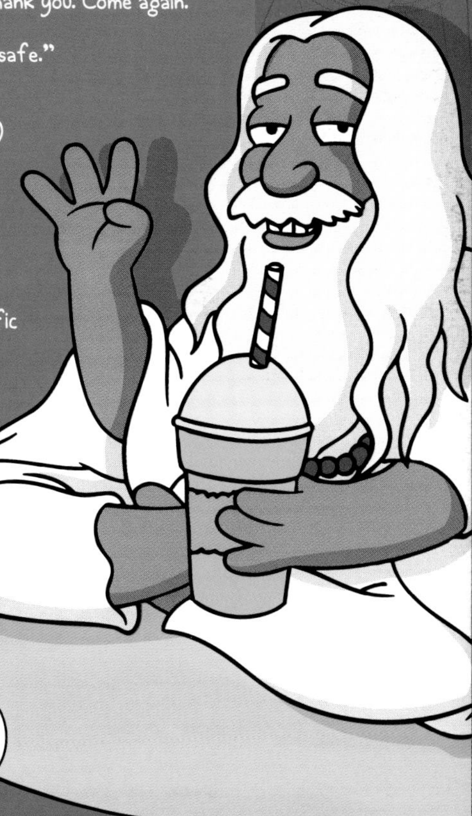

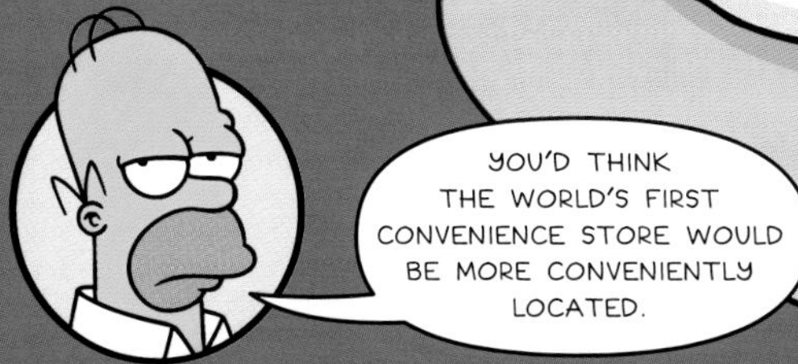
YOU'D THINK THE WORLD'S FIRST CONVENIENCE STORE WOULD BE MORE CONVENIENTLY LOCATED.

# THE MANY MUTA

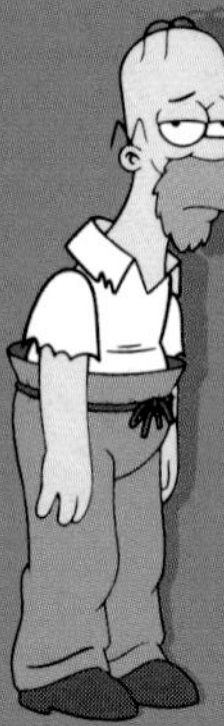

HUNGRY HUNGRY HOMER

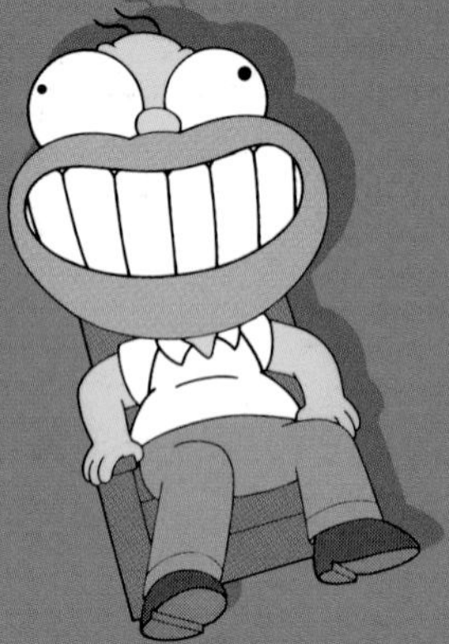

VACUUM-HEAD HOMER

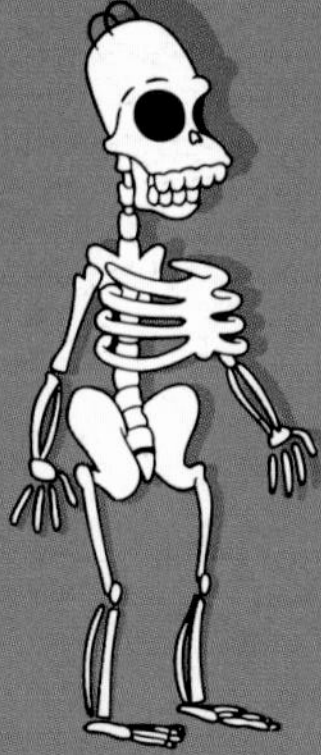

BARE BONES HOMER

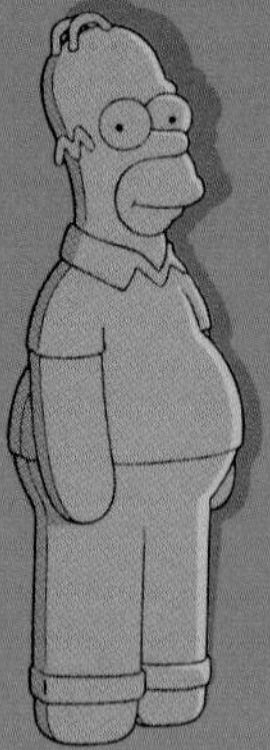

GINGERBREAD HOMER

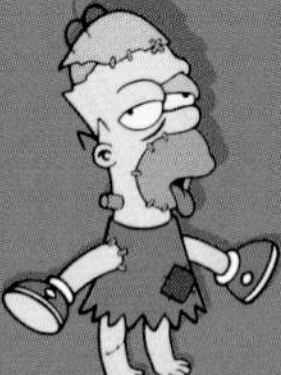

PATCHWORK HOMER

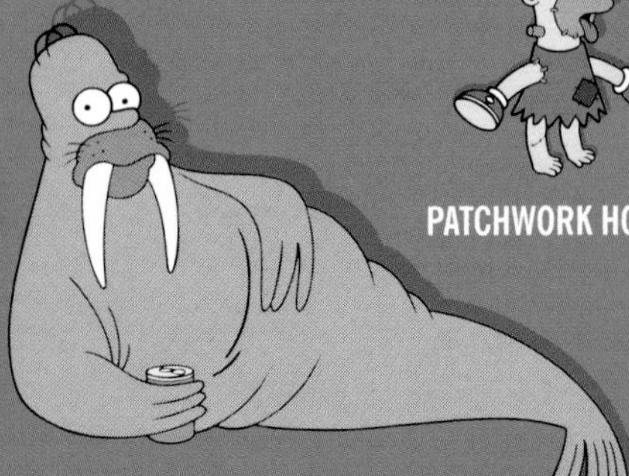

(I AM THE WALRUS) HOMER

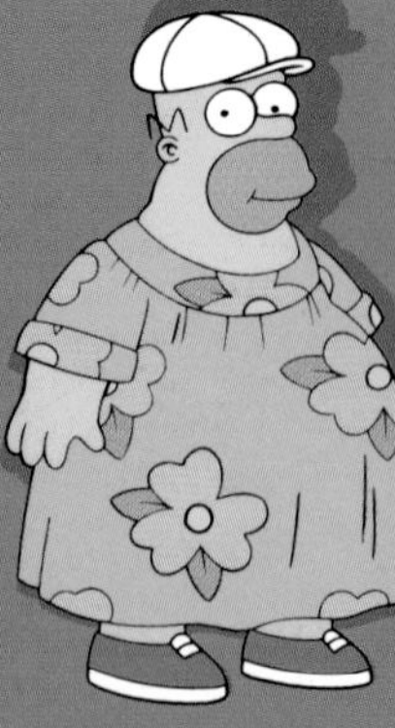

KING-SIZE HOMER

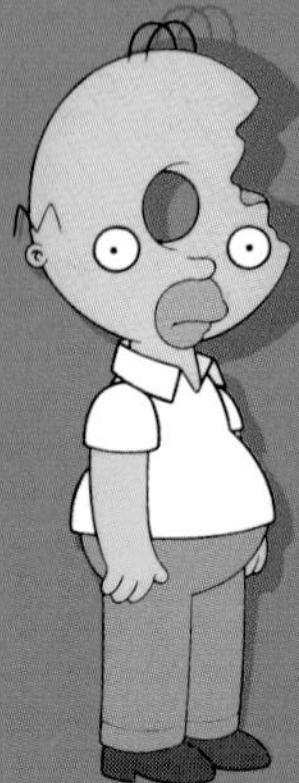

DONUT HEAD HOMER

# TIONS OF HOMER

**INSIDE-OUT HOMER**

**KING HOMER**

**BIGFOOT HOMER**

**HOMER-IN-THE-BOX**

**FERTILIZING HOMER**

**HOMER MUNSTER**

**GENDER-CONFUSED HOMER**

**HOMERBOT**

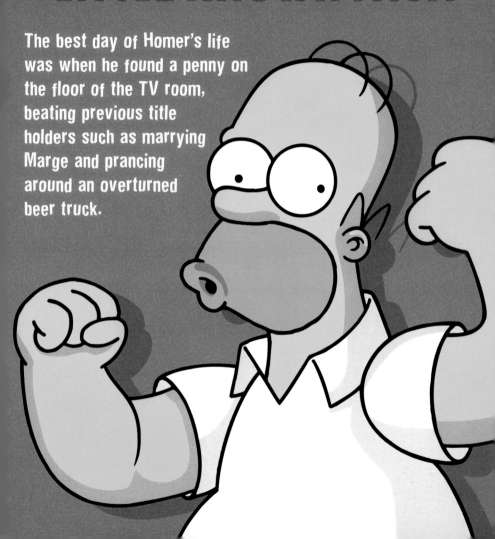

# LITTLE KNOWN FACT:

The best day of Homer's life was when he found a penny on the floor of the TV room, beating previous title holders such as marrying Marge and prancing around an overturned beer truck.

# Homer's Heroes

## KNIGHTBOAT

The weekly TV adventures of Knightboat keep Homer on the edge of his seat, despite disparaging comments by Marge.

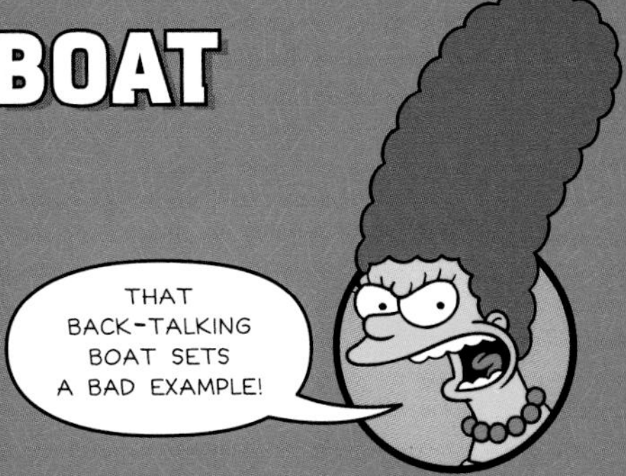
THAT BACK-TALKING BOAT SETS A BAD EXAMPLE!

Also known as: The crime-solving boat.

Specializes in: Catching starfish poachers.

Driven by: Muscular pessimist Michael.

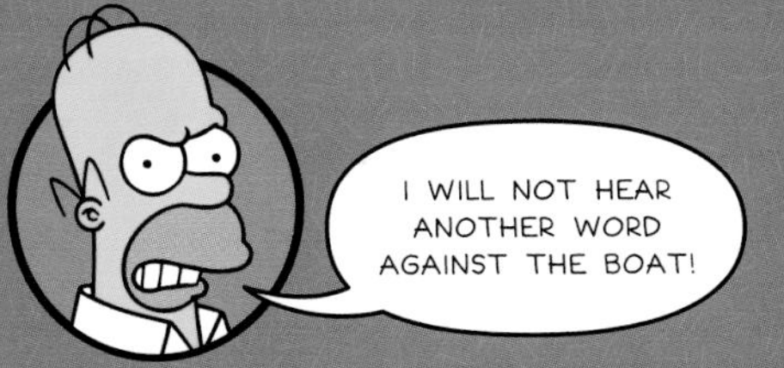
I WILL NOT HEAR ANOTHER WORD AGAINST THE BOAT!

Access to land: Canals, inlets, and fjords.

Voice: Gentle, yet firm; wise, yet annoying.

Lasting evidence of Homer's loyalty: Photo of Knightboat on TV in family photo album.

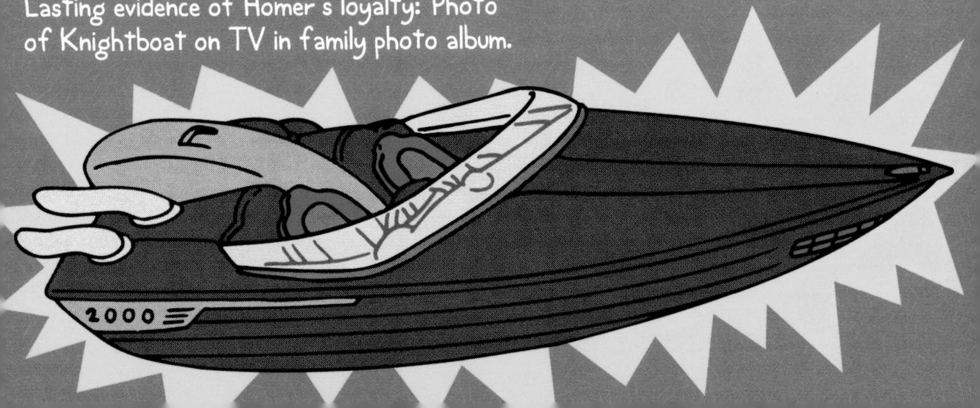
2000

# A TYPICAL DAY IN THE LIFE

7:00 a.m. - Homer wakes with funny taste in his mouth. He dreamed about sucking raspberry filling out of giant donuts.

7:05 a.m. - Discovers new tube of raspberry-flavored toothpaste in bathroom is half-empty.

7:15 a.m. - Eats entire package of graham crackers topped with remaining raspberry toothpaste.

7:30 a.m. - Takes lengthy shower, sings most of libretto from "Tommy" by The Who. Coincidentally, chokes on water and gets soap in both eyes during "deaf, dumb, and blind" part.

8:00 a.m. - Time to get dressed. After several minutes weighing pros and cons, decides to wear blue pants and white shirt.

8:15 a.m. - Breakfast is served! Mmmm...bacon, eggs, sausage, toast and waffles. Pleasant mood is interrupted when Bart and Lisa argue about price of tea in China. Homer angrily pounds table with fist, causing one of his plump sausages to go flying onto floor.

8:16 a.m. - In panic to rescue rolling sausage, Homer stabs at floor with fork. Accidentally stabs the tip of Snowball II's tail. Spontaneous cat clawing follows, from Homer's chin to forehead.

9:00 a.m. - After dropping Snowball II off at veterinarian, Marge drives Homer to emergency room. Homer sobs into bloody towel about "his face, his beautiful face."

9:15 a.m. - Dr. Hibbert and emergency room staff get quite a few chuckles from cat scratches on Homer's forehead—they form an image closely resembling state Springfield is in.

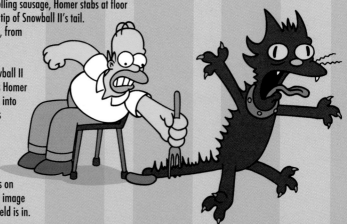

# OF HOMER SIMPSON

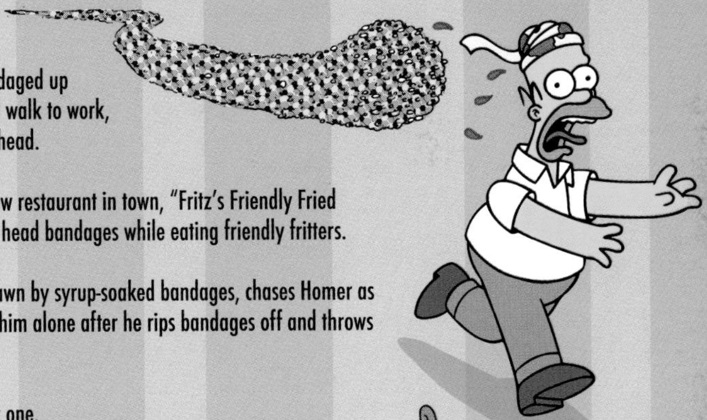

9:30 a.m. – Extremely irritated, Homer leaves hospital with his entire face bandaged up like The Mummy. He tells Marge he will walk to work, since she is still giggling about his forehead.

9:40 a.m. – Stops to have brunch at new restaurant in town, "Fritz's Friendly Fried Fritters." Gets maple syrup all over his head bandages while eating friendly fritters.

10:00 a.m. – Swarm of honeybees, drawn by syrup-soaked bandages, chases Homer as he exits restaurant. They finally leave him alone after he rips bandages off and throws them to homeless person.

10:05 a.m. – Slips into Moe's for quick one.

11:00 a.m. – Pair of paramedics stop into Moe's for a liquid lunch. Fisticuffs ensue when one paramedic notices Homer's forehead and asks if "he's the new State Dork."

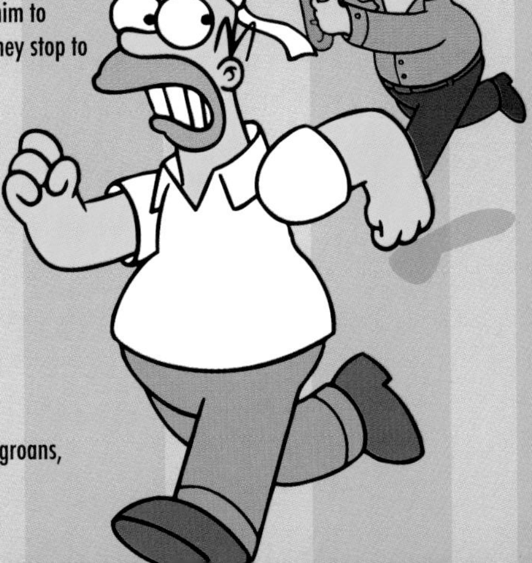

11:10 a.m. – Paramedics give Homer a beat-down, then drive him to emergency room. Hospital staff happily welcomes him back. They stop to take pictures of his forehead for their scrapbook.

11:25 a.m. – Re-bandaged, Homer takes taxi back to Moe's.

11:40 a.m. – Wounded, unable to see, and quite tipsy, Homer mistakes King Toot's Music Store for Moe's men's room. Takes wizz on Wurlitzer.

11:45 a.m. – King Toot's owner chases Homer down street, trying to clobber him with trombone.

11:50 a.m. – Homer's appearance, along with his swaggering groans, frightens Mrs. Rooney's first-grade class while on walking field trip to City Hall. Some children are missing for hours.

12:00 p.m. – Shows up for work just in time for lunch. Today's special: Barbecue Surprise.

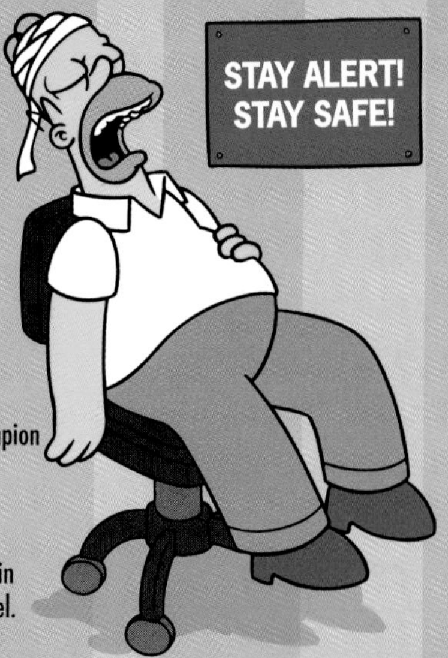
STAY ALERT!
STAY SAFE!

12:15 p.m. – Everyone in lunchroom wants to know what happened to his face. Homer describes how he saved orphanage from hungry wolves–in graphic detail.

12:40 p.m. – Bandages are splattered with Barbecue Surprise sauce. He mistakenly enters ladies' room and removes them, except for one that covers his forehead.

12:50 p.m. – Homer realizes he's in ladies' room when Radon Specialist Isadora "The Moose" Brauvonovitch, 6′ 4″ former women's shot-put champion for Soviet bloc, comes out of stall and delivers right hook to his chin. When he comes to, she makes pass at him.

1:00 p.m. – Lunchtime over, Homer challenges Lenny to electric cart race in Sector 8-C. He loses control on third lap, crashes into coolant exhaust panel.

1:15 p.m. – Coolant exhaust alarms clear factory. Homer, Lenny, Carl, and Charlie shoot craps in the parking lot.

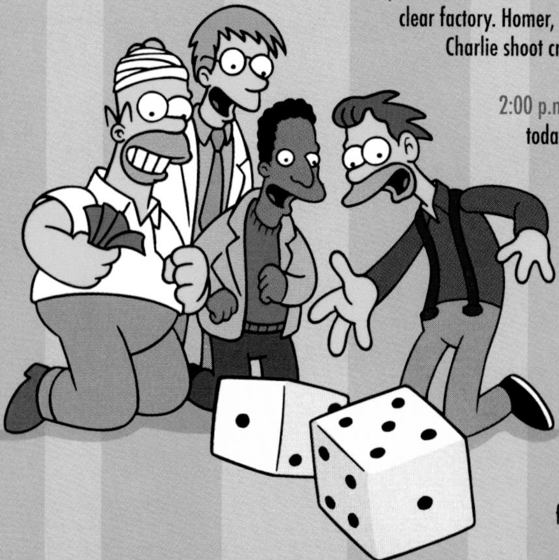

2:00 p.m. – Returning to his workstation for first time today, Homer accidentally erases all his phone messages. Most of them were from Mr. Burns.

2:10 p.m. – Makes prank phone calls. Most of them are to Mr. Burns.

3:00 p.m. – Naptime.

4:00 p.m. – Donuts and coffee break. Homer remains in break room until it is time to clock out.

5:10 p.m. – Homer, Lenny, and Carl stop by Moe's for after-work aperitif–or two.

6:00 p.m. – Remembers to stop by Kwik-E-Mart to pick up some things for Marge.

6:05 p.m. – Eats Bucket-O-Microwave Ravioli.

6:10 p.m. – Returns to Kwik-E-Mart when he remembers he forgot to pick up some things for Marge.

6:15 p.m. – Eats Tub-O-Corndogs.

7:00 p.m. – Home in time for dinner. Marge nags him for forgetting the things she asked him to pick up at store. Snowball II hisses at him, favoring tip of her tail which is wrapped in bandage.

7:30 p.m. – Homer and Bart enjoy a little father/son bonding. They repeatedly ring Flanders' doorbell and run away.

8:00 p.m. – Family TV time. Tonight's movie fare: "The Man with a Thousand Face Scratches," starring Troy McClure. Many comparisons, gigglings, and temper flares ensue.

9:00 p.m. – During commercial, kids try to see what is under Homer's forehead bandage. He refuses, but they pursue him all over house. He hides in treehouse until they go to sleep.

9:30 p.m. – Homer decides to ring Flanders' doorbell one more time. While running away, gets hit in street by ambulance driven by drunk paramedics. Homer talks them into going to Moe's instead of hospital.

10:50 p.m. – Paramedics drop Homer off at home. He doesn't remember why, but he has a trombone wrapped around his neck.

11:00 p.m. – Ten intimate minutes with Marge.

11:10 p.m. – Glad day is finally over, Homer gratefully drifts off to sleep.

11:12 p.m. – Maggie rips bandage off Homer's forehead to see what is underneath. She laughs at what she sees. Homer screams in pain.

# HOMER'S '70s CRASH PAD

1. Pink Floyd "Dark Side of the Moon" poster (won from Barney in "The Superbowl of Chinese Football").
2. Pressboard "peace sign" made in AP Woodshop.
3. Ultra-melty candle.
4. S.A.T. prep book (unopened).
5. Nattering Nabob Brand X-tra Wide Low-Rise Bell Bottoms.
6. Puma sneakers.
7. Patriotic "peace sign" rug.
8. Springfield Squatters Cap (name later changed to "Isotopes").
9. 52 thread count sheets.
10. Lamp with black lightbulb.
11. Black light Led Zepplin poster (important symbol of commitment to "rocking hard")
12. Pet Rock.
13. Abe's hand-me-down lucky drinking sweater.
14. JCPenney's wood veneer four poster bed.
15. Empty beer can collection (concealing a six pack of full cans).
16. Springfield Civic Pride Pennant (found in the trash outside of the Quimby house).
17. The Rock Pit (area reserved for serious rocking, featuring: beanbag chair, headphones, quad-stereo system, LPs and 8-Track tapes, including Grand Funk Railroad "On Time," Deep Purple "Machine Head," Alice Cooper "Billion Dollar Babies," and Ray Stevens "Gitarzan").
18. Lava lamp stain.

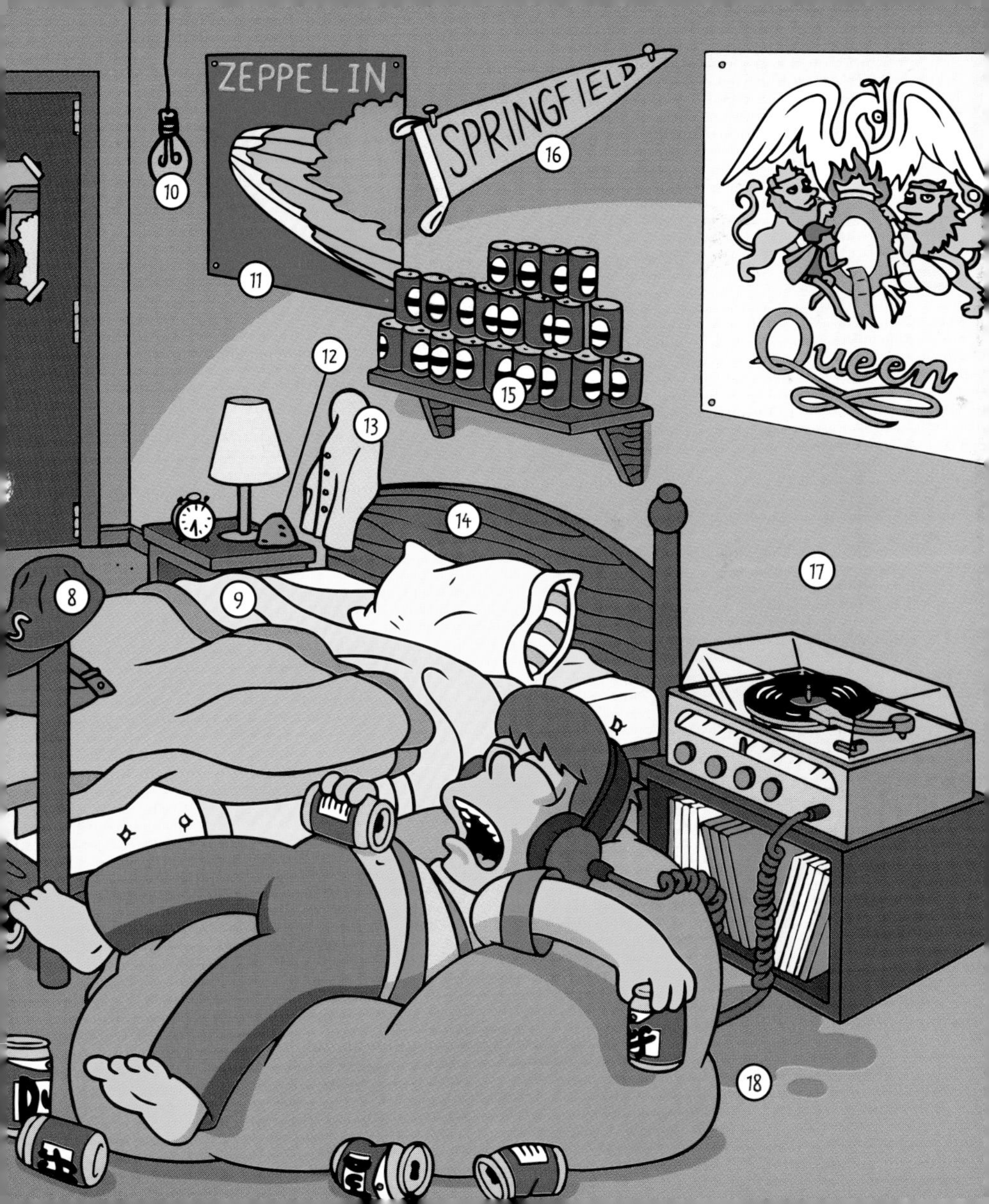

ZEPPELIN
SPRINGFIELD
Queen
8
9
10
11
12
13
14
15
16
17
18

# '70s HOMER SIMPSON STUDENT/UNDERACHIEVER

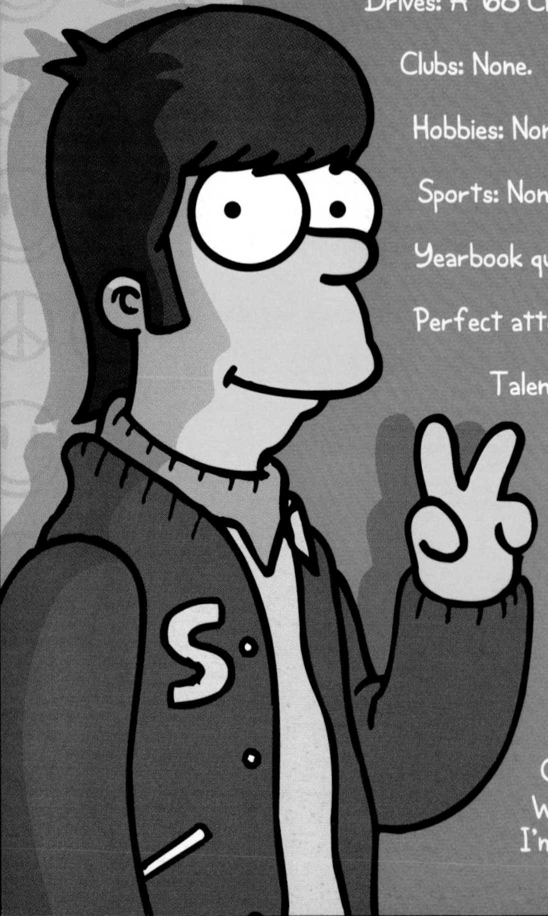

Favorite Song: "The Joker" by The Steve Miller Band.

Favorite Band: Grand Funk Railroad.

Drives: A '68 Charger w/chain link steering wheel.

Clubs: None.

Hobbies: None.

Sports: None.

Yearbook quote: "Ah, so many memories!"

Perfect attendance: Detention Room.

Talent: Making phony hall passes.

Greatest ambition: To marry Marge Bouvier

Voted "Most Likely to": Be responsible for some kind of natural or technological disaster.

Reason for slim figure: High metabomalism.

Quote: "English Class? Who needs that? I'm never going to England."

# ‘70s MARGE BOUVIER HOMER’S FIRST CRUSH

Favorite Book: “Jonathan Livingston Seagull”

Favorite magazine: “Ms.”

Biggest worry: The city forensics finals.

Believes in: Equal Rights, unless there’s heavy lifting or Math involved.

Yearbook quote: “If you can’t say something nice, say it in French.”

Hobbies: Painting, making jewelry out of soda can pull tabs.

Clubs: Future Obedient Housewives of Springfield and S.C.O.W.L. (Springfield Club for Outraged Women’s Libbers).

Sports: Varsity Bake-off, Jai Alai.

Greatest Ambition: To meet Ringo Starr in person.

Voted “Most Likely to”: Marry beneath her.

Quote: “Your French is tres bien!”

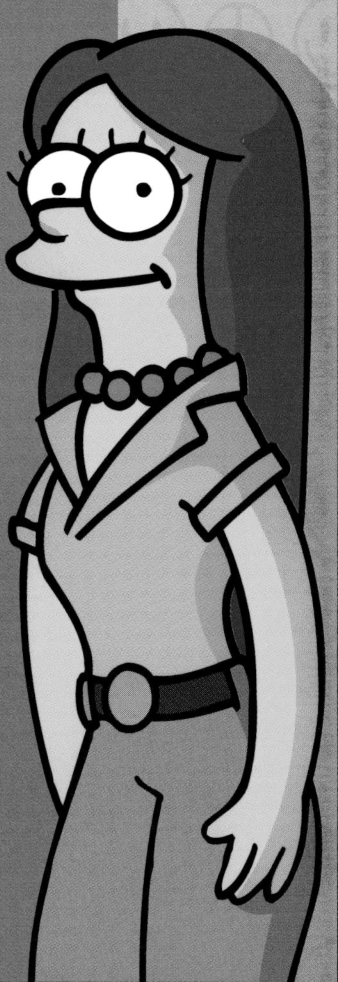

# '70s PRINCIPAL DONDELINGER HOMER'S HIGH SCHOOL PRINCIPAL

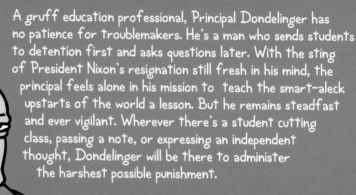

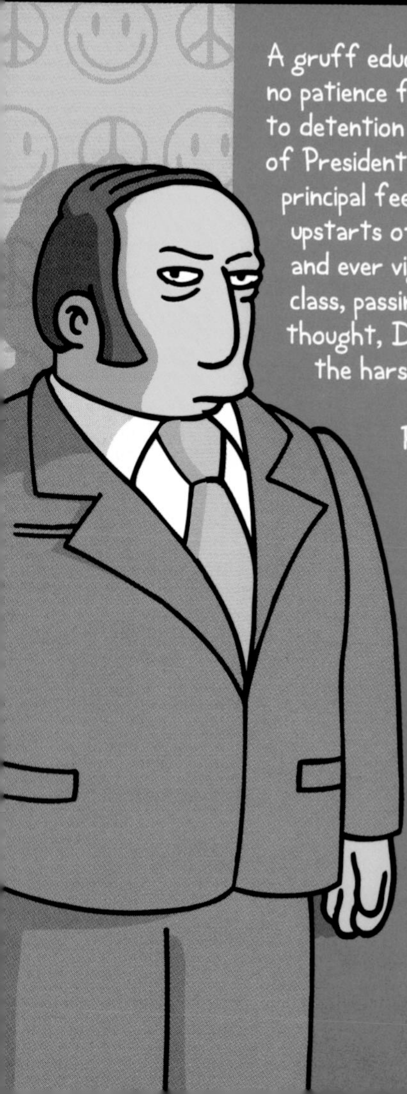

A gruff education professional, Principal Dondelinger has no patience for troublemakers. He's a man who sends students to detention first and asks questions later. With the sting of President Nixon's resignation still fresh in his mind, the principal feels alone in his mission to teach the smart-aleck upstarts of the world a lesson. But he remains steadfast and ever vigilant. Wherever there's a student cutting class, passing a note, or expressing an independent thought, Dondelinger will be there to administer the harshest possible punishment.

Range of emotions: Frustration to stern disapproval.

Winner of: The 1973 Princey Award for Best Principal.

Likes: The mellow musical stylings of Elton John.

Dislikes: Streakers at the prom.

Secret dream: To make the cover of "Disciplinarian Illustrated" magazine.

Quote: "Well, well, well, if it isn't Homer Simpson and Barney Gumble, Springfield's answer to Cheech and Chong!"

Part-time job: Pin polisher at Barney's Bowl-A-Rama.

Sports: After-School Varsity Penny-Pitching Team.

Clubs: Bob Fosse Tap Dance Appreciation Society.

Yearbook quote: "I swear I had pants on when I got here!"

Talent: Can belch the lead guitar riff from "Smoke on the Water."

Ambitions: To work for the Space Program or become a world-famous brain surgeon.

Voted "Most Likely to": Talk to leprechauns.

Quote: "Okay, Homer, I'll try a beer... but just this once!"

Worst debating moment: Being mooned for "Re-Butt-al" by Homer Simpson.

Yearbook quote: "Today, we stand on the threshold of tomorrow's doorway to the future."

Clubs: Debating Society, Chess Club, Backgammon Club, Model U.N., Drama League, Latin Association, Shakespeare Guild, Glee Club, Future Wine-tasters of America.

Other activities: Yearbook Committee, Color Guard, Cheerleading Squad, Hall Monitor, Official Teacher's Pet.

Honors: Class Valedictorian, Perfect Attendance Award (K-12), Winner of Spirit Week "Biggest Afro" Contest.

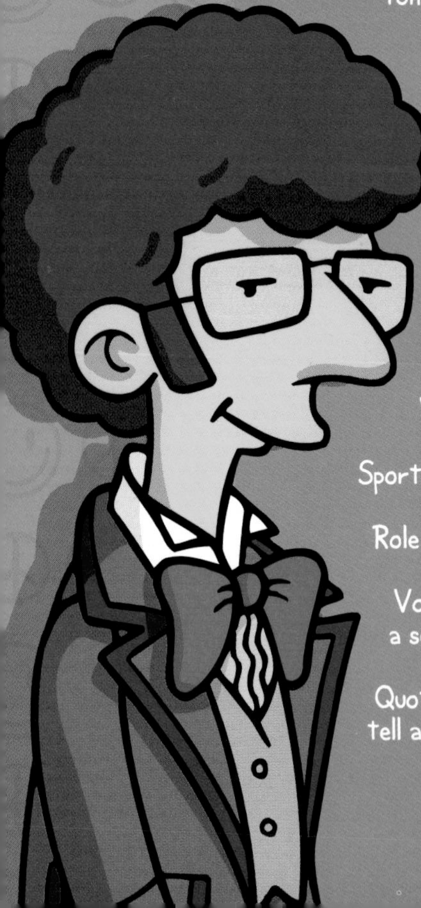

Sports: Polo, Human Chess Board (King).

Role model: Himself.

Voted "Most Likely to": Have the means to settle a sexual harassment suit out of court.

Quote: "I would appreciate it if you didn't tell anybody about my busy hands."

# '70s PATTY & SELMA BOUVIER HOMER'S FUTURE SISTERS-IN-LAW

Status: Springfield High alumni.

High School clubs: Future Bureaucrats Club, Young Women's Herpetology Association.

Yearbook quotation:
(Patty) "It has always been my rule never to smoke when asleep, and never to refrain when awake." – Mark Twain.
(Selma) "Why do you build me up, buttercup, baby, just to let me down?"– The Foundations.

Favorite magazine: "Tiger Beat" (Selma for the pictures, Patty for the articles).

Hobbies: Smoking Laramie Hi-Tar cigarettes, grunting, Polaroid photography.

Voices: Raspy (even then).

Strange quirk: They always answer the door together.

Twin thing: Finishing each other's sentences.

Future male in their lives: Jub Jub.

Quote: (Selma) "Marge's dates get homelier all the time."
(Patty) "That's what you get when you don't put out."

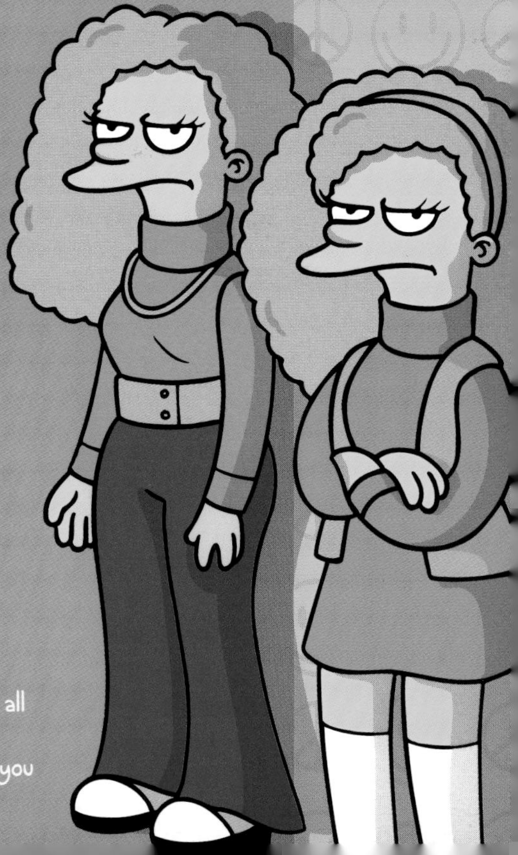

So far out, your brain will boogie!
So psychedelic, your aura will wriggle!
So unreadable, your eyes will throb! It's...

# ...HOMER'S POSTER PIT

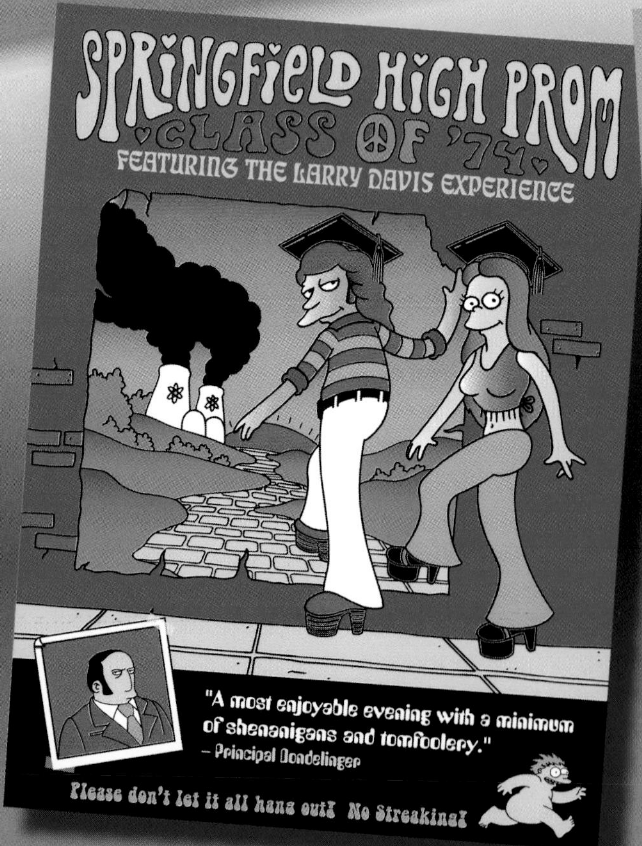
SPRINGFIELD HIGH PROM
CLASS OF '74
FEATURING THE LARRY DAVIS EXPERIENCE
"A most enjoyable evening with a minimum of shenanigans and tomfoolery."
– Principal Dondelinger
Please don't let it all hang out! No Streaking!

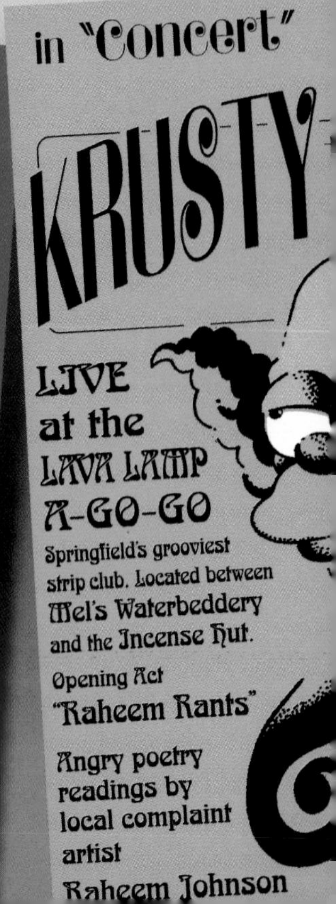
in "Concert"
KRUSTY
LIVE
at the
LAVA LAMP
A-GO-GO
Springfield's grooviest strip club. Located between Mel's Waterbeddery and the Incense Hut.
Opening Act
"Raheem Rants"
Angry poetry readings by local complaint artist
Raheem Johnson

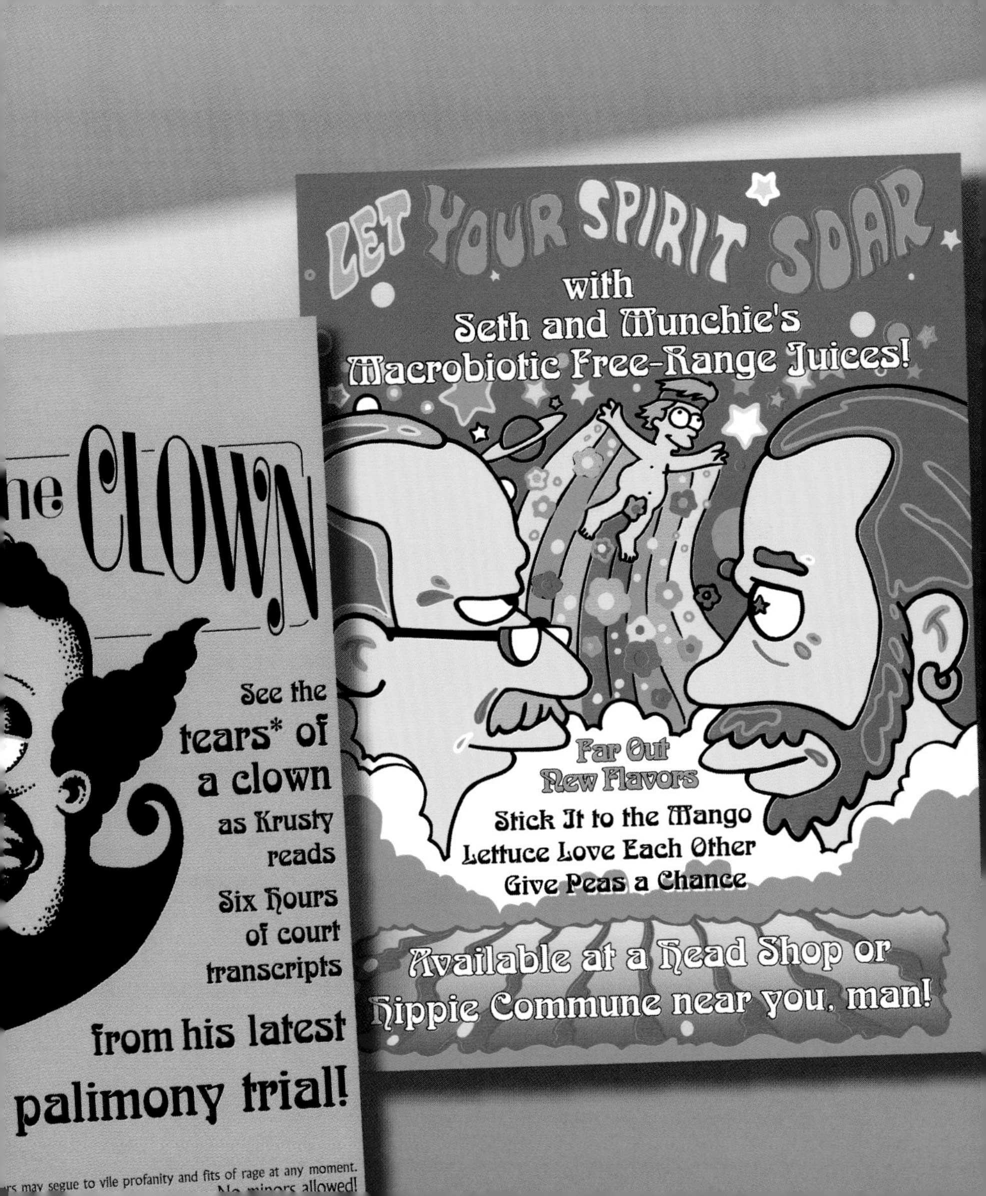

CLOWN
See the tears* of a clown as Krusty reads Six Hours of court transcripts from his latest palimony trial!
may segue to vile profanity and fits of rage at any moment.
No minors allowed!
LET YOUR SPIRIT SOAR
with Seth and Munchie's Macrobiotic Free-Range Juices!
Far Out New Flavors
Stick It to the Mango
Lettuce Love Each Other
Give Peas a Chance
Available at a Head Shop or Hippie Commune near you, man!

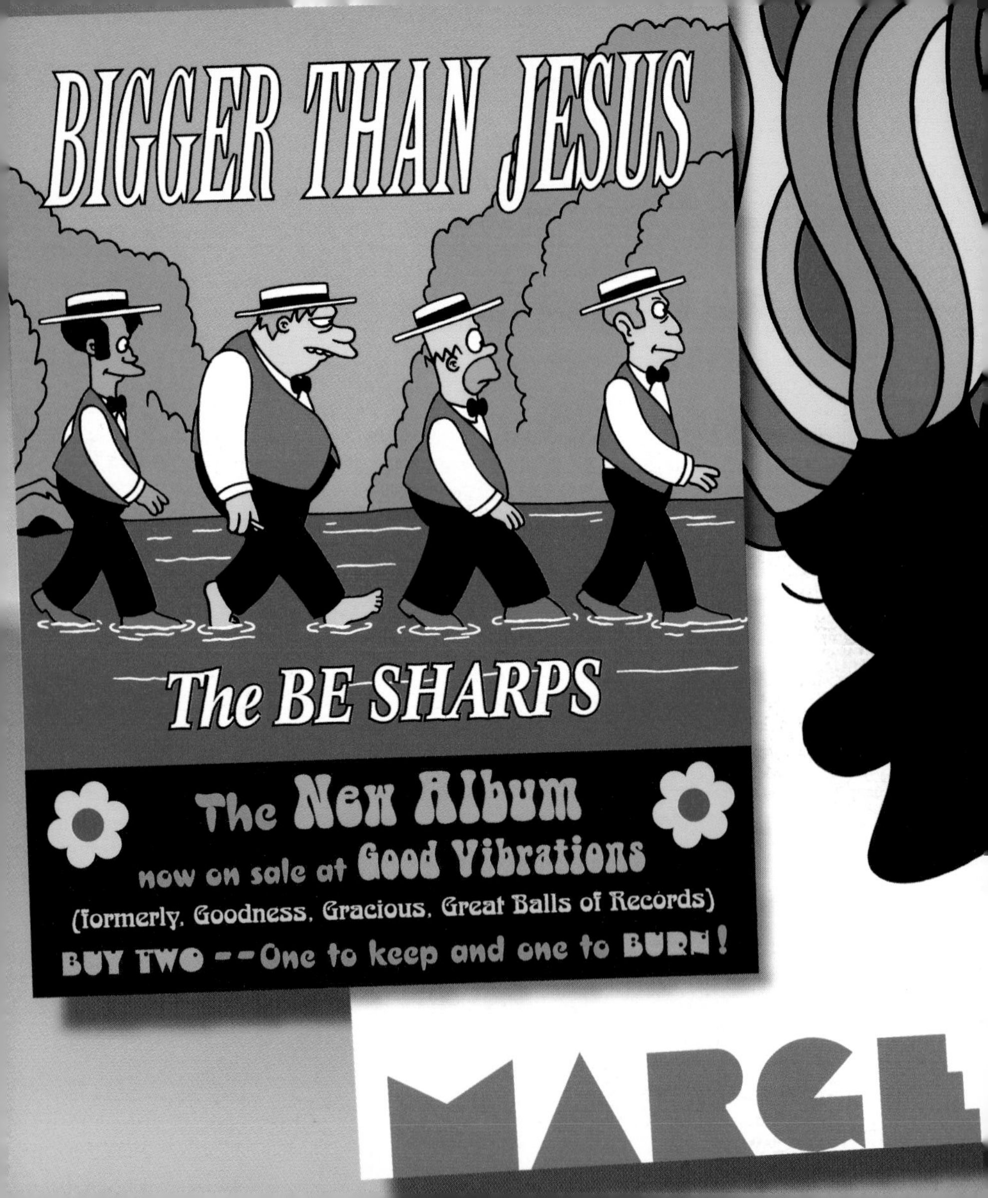
BIGGER THAN JESUS
The BE SHARPS
The New Album
now on sale at Good Vibrations
(formerly, Goodness, Gracious, Great Balls of Records)
BUY TWO --One to keep and one to BURN!
MARG

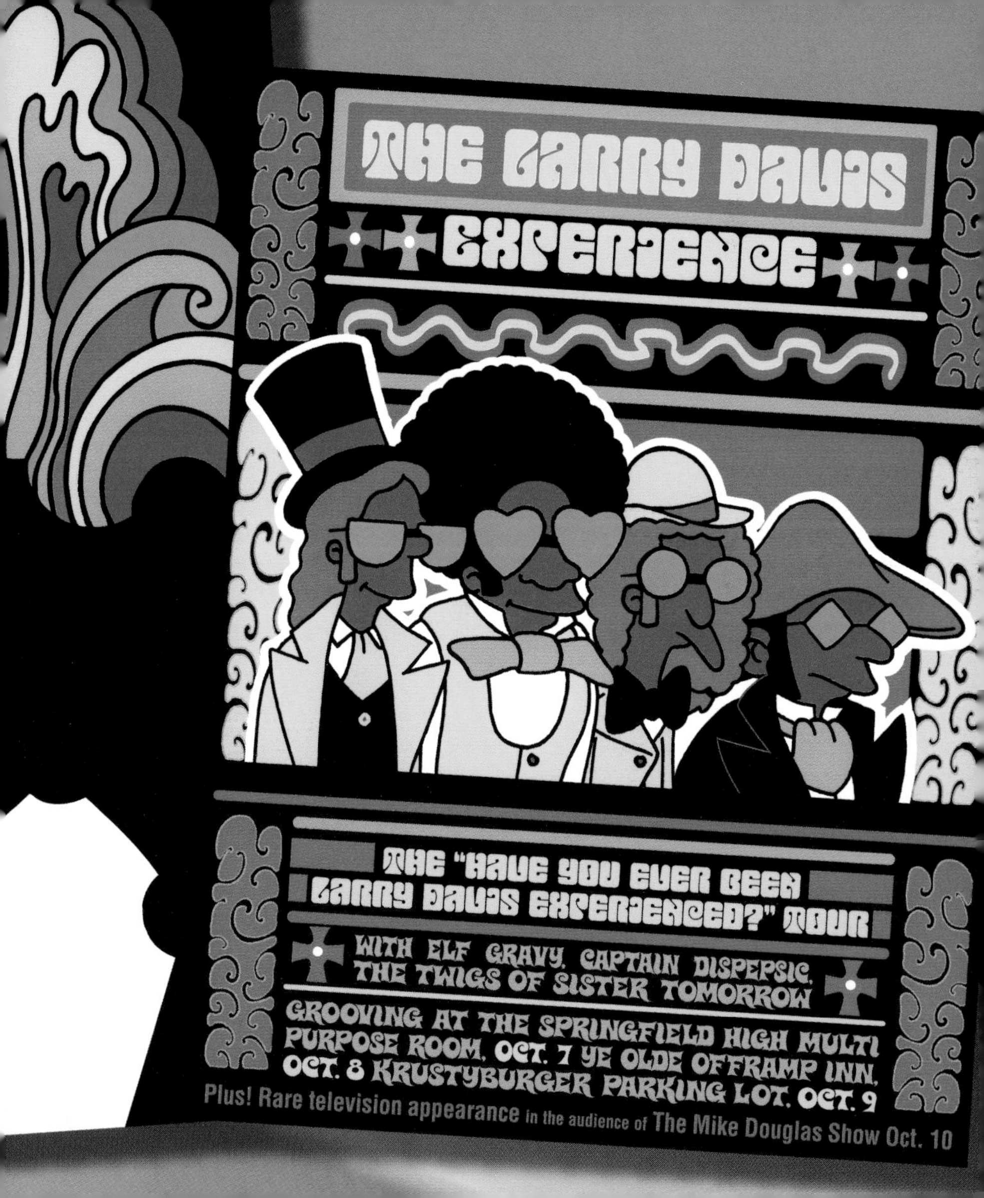
THE LARRY DAVIS
EXPERIENCE
THE "HAVE YOU EVER BEEN
LARRY DAVIS EXPERIENCED?" TOUR
WITH ELF GRAVY, CAPTAIN DISPEPSIC,
THE TWIGS OF SISTER TOMORROW
GROOVING AT THE SPRINGFIELD HIGH MULTI
PURPOSE ROOM, OCT. 7 YE OLDE OFFRAMP INN,
OCT. 8 KRUSTYBURGER PARKING LOT, OCT. 9
Plus! Rare television appearance in the audience of The Mike Douglas Show Oct. 10

# THE HAIRCLUB

"THE LOVE PIRATE"

"THE STRAY CAT"

"THE INCREDIBLE HULK"

"EL VATO"

"THE DESPERATE YEARS"

"THE JOHN BIRCH"

# FOR HOMER___

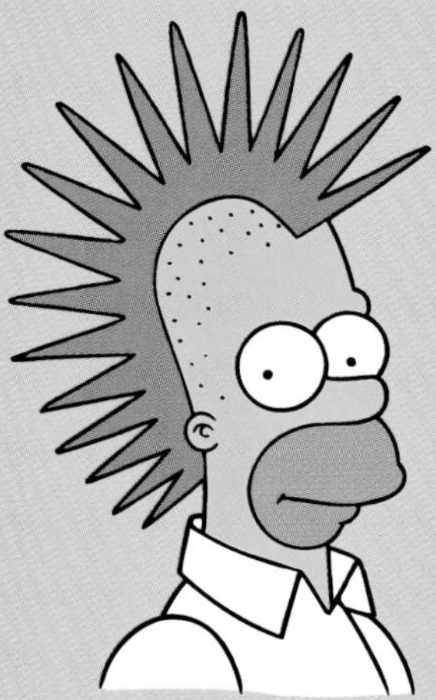

"MOM'S WORST NIGHTMARE"

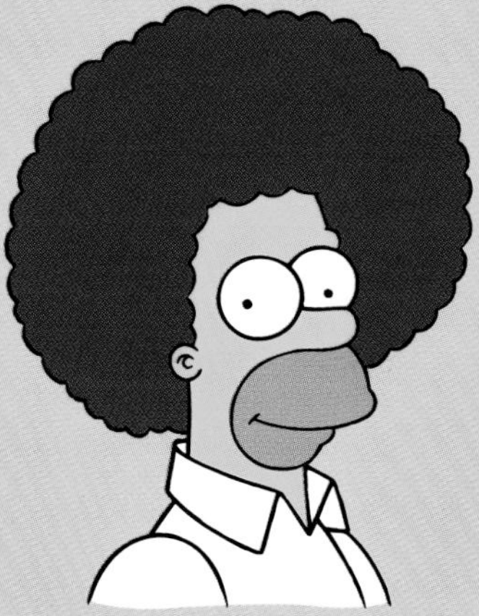

"THE NATURAL"

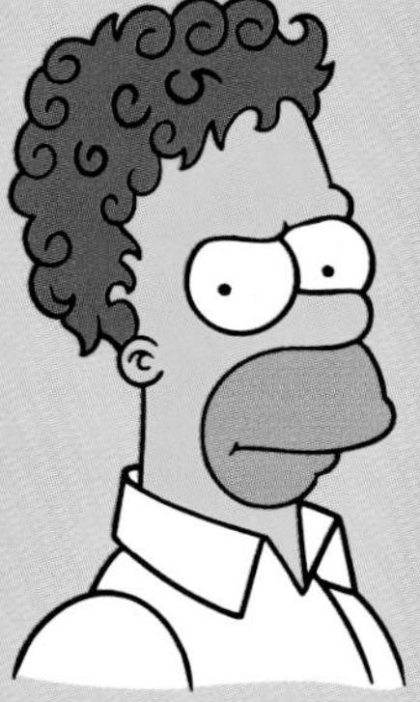

"THE MIKE BRADY"

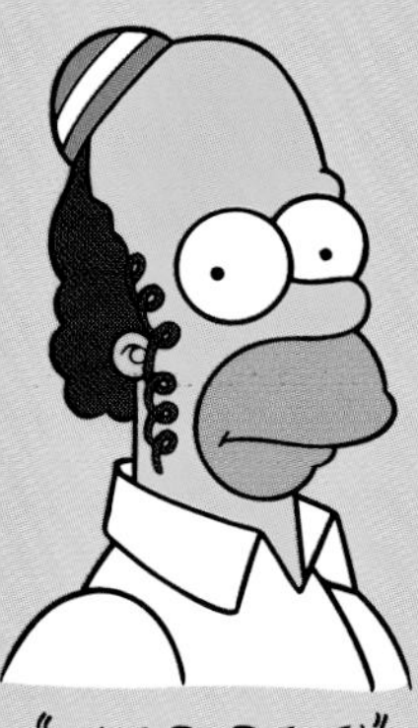

"THE BUBELEH"

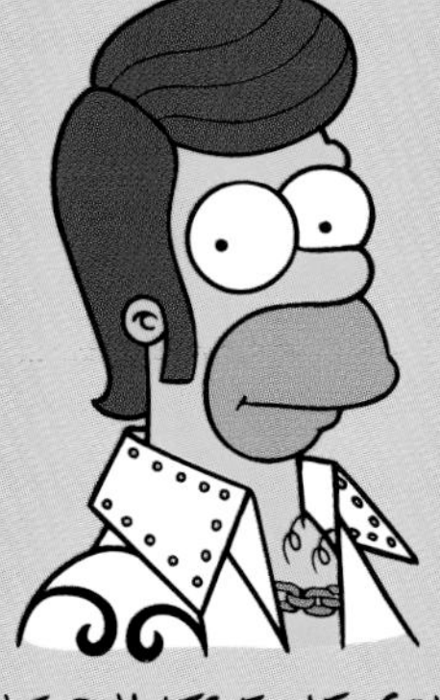

"THE RHINESTONE COWBOY"

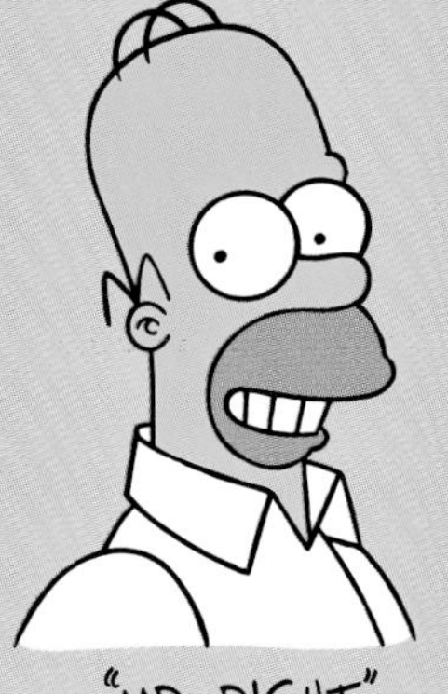

"MR. RIGHT"

# LITTLE KNOWN FACT:

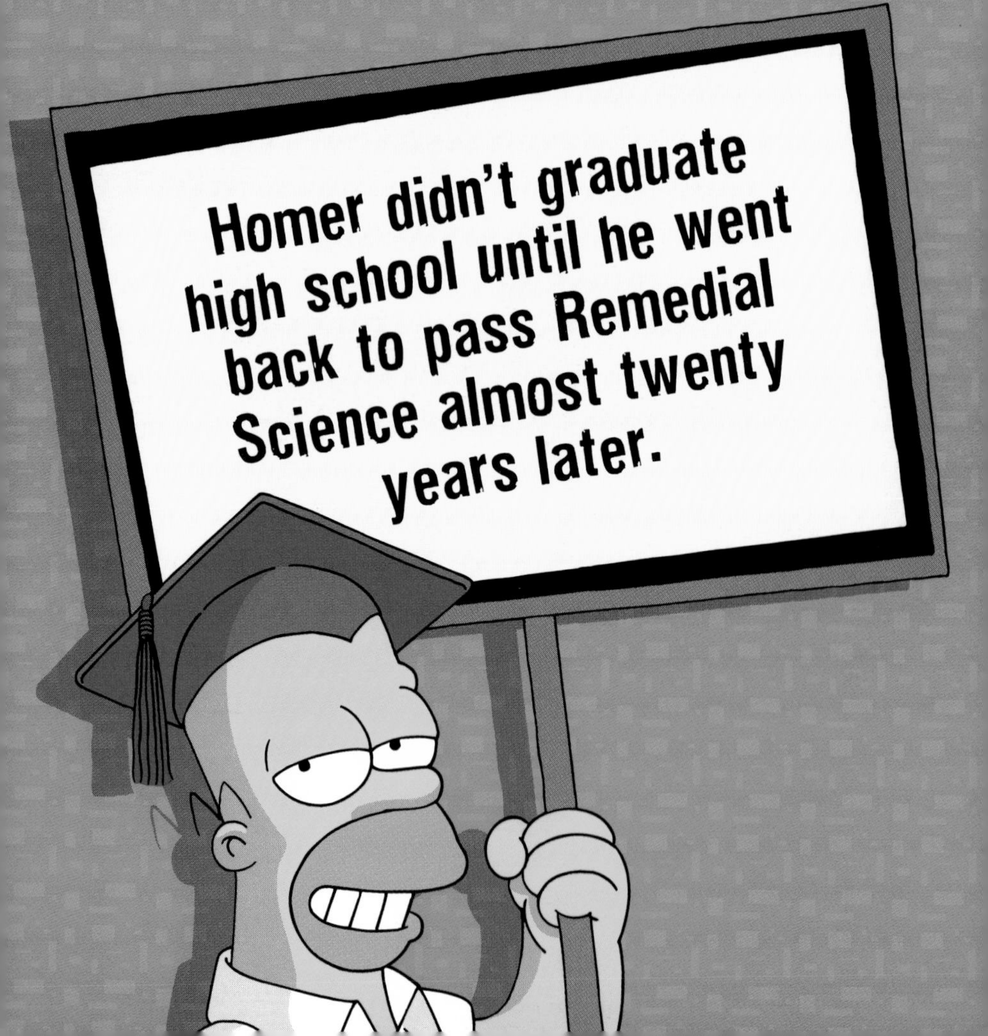
Homer didn't graduate high school until he went back to pass Remedial Science almost twenty years later.

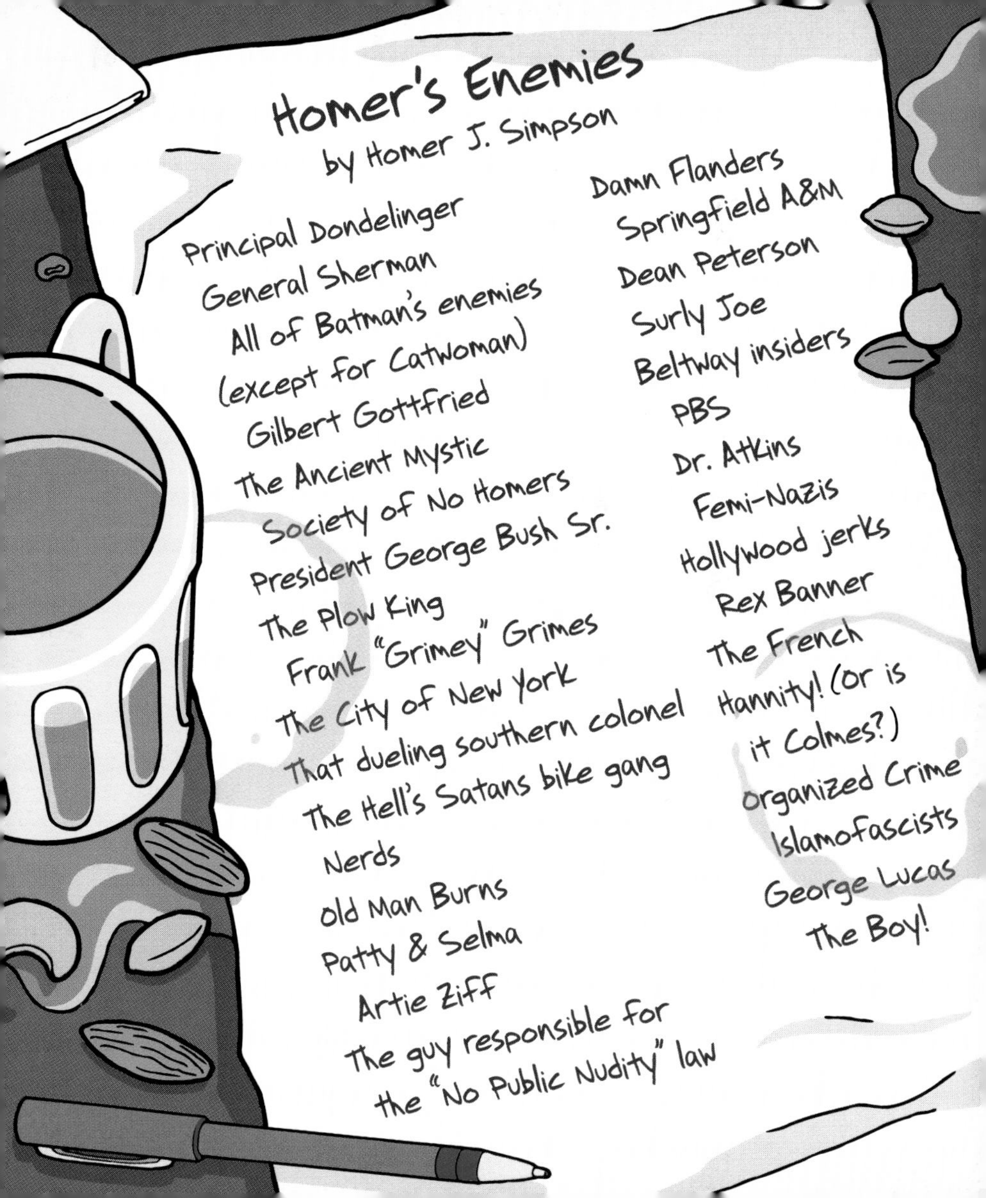
Homer's Enemies
by Homer J. Simpson
Principal Dondelinger
General Sherman
All of Batman's enemies
(except for Catwoman)
Gilbert Gottfried
The Ancient Mystic
Society of No Homers
President George Bush Sr.
The Plow King
Frank "Grimey" Grimes
The City of New York
That dueling southern colonel
The Hell's Satans bike gang
Nerds
Old Man Burns
Patty & Selma
Artie Ziff
The guy responsible for
the "No Public Nudity" law
Damn Flanders
Springfield A&M
Dean Peterson
Surly Joe
Beltway insiders
PBS
Dr. Atkins
Femi-Nazis
Hollywood jerks
Rex Banner
The French
Hannity! (Or is
it Colmes?)
Organized Crime
Islamofascists
George Lucas
The Boy!

# THE MANY *more* MUTA

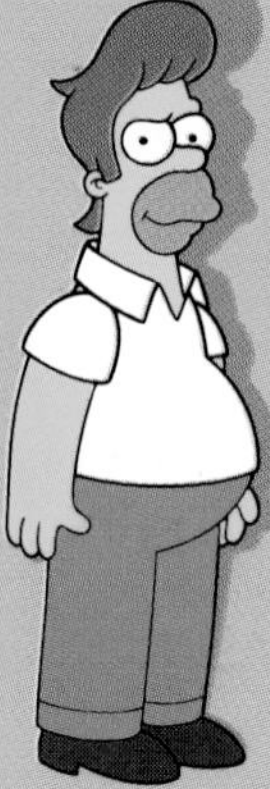

SNAKE-HAIR HOMER

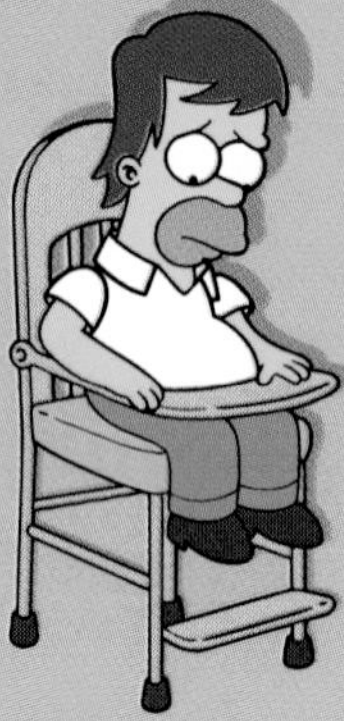

TINY TOT HOMER

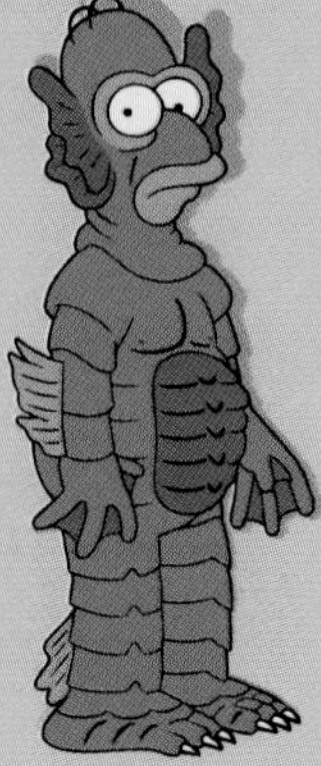

THE HOMER FROM THE BLACK LAGOON

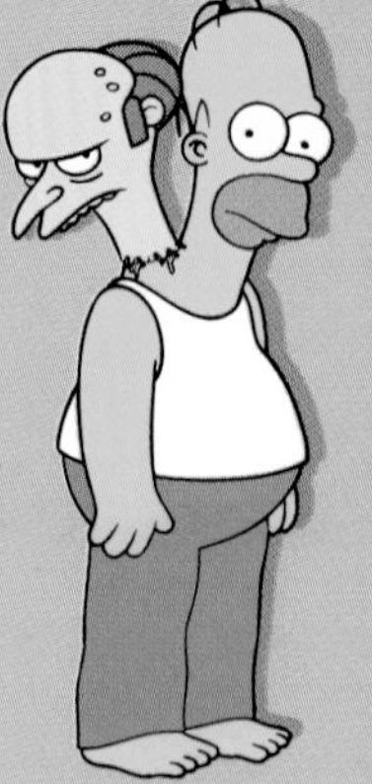

THE INCREDIBLE TWO-HEADED HOMER

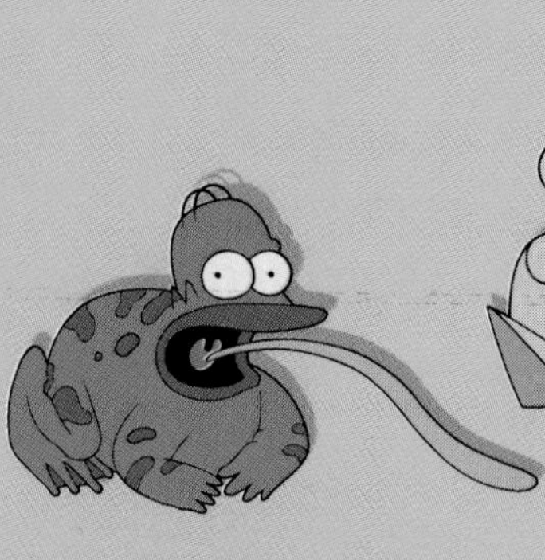

WARTS AND ALL HOMER

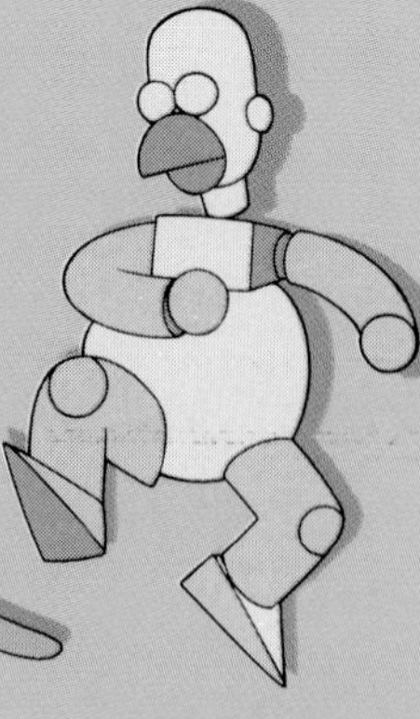

GEOMETRIC HOMER

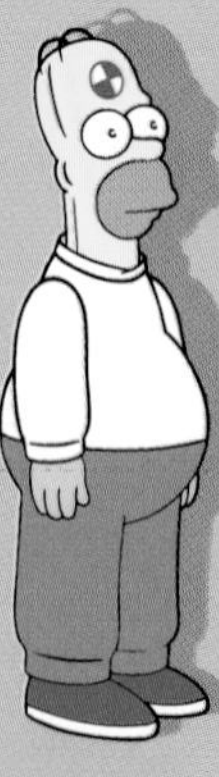

CRASH TEST HOMER

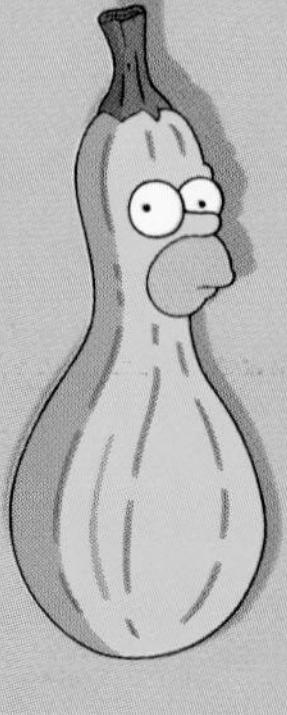

HOME-GROWN HOMER

# TIONS OF HOMER

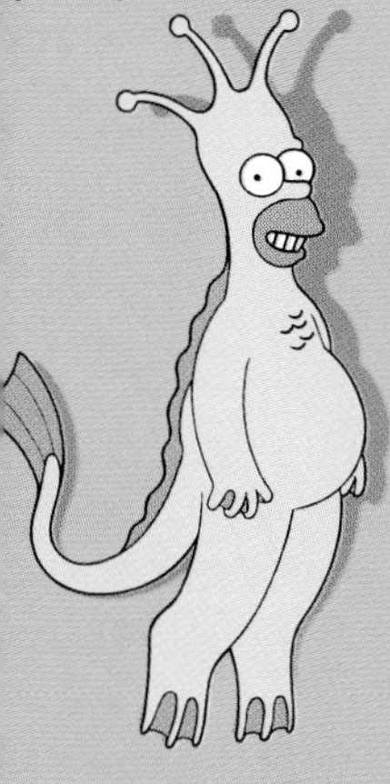

SEA MONKEY HOMER

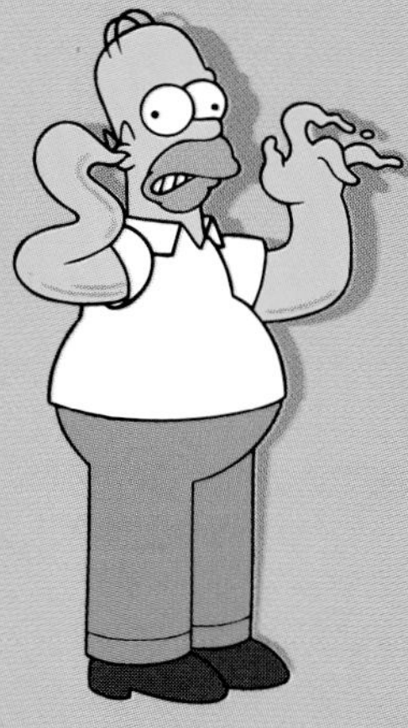

HALLUCINOGENIC HOMER

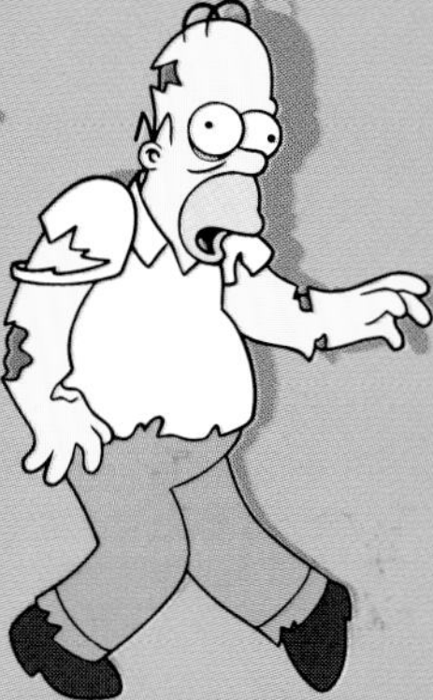

ZOMBIE HOMER

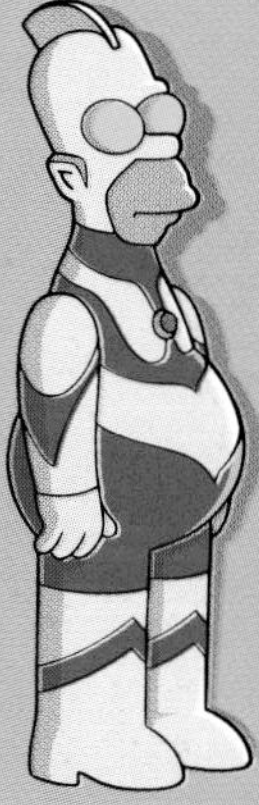

ANIME HOMER

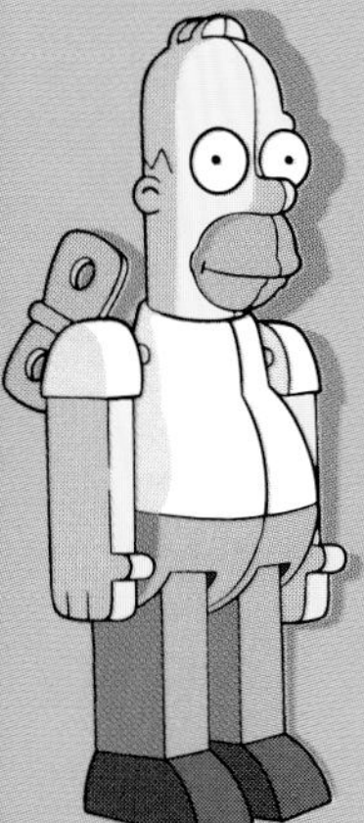

WIND-UP HOMER

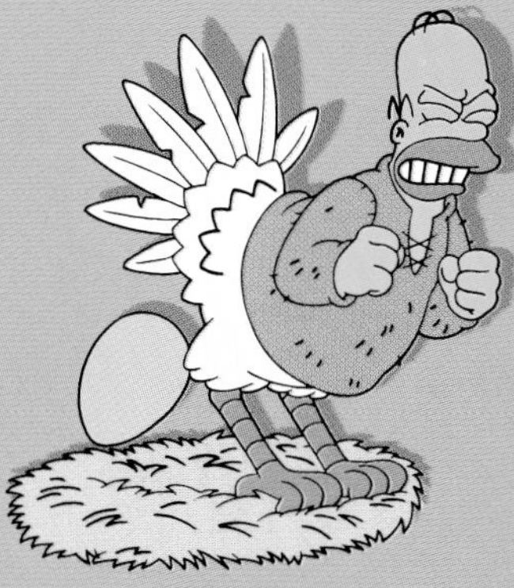

HENNY PENNY HOMER

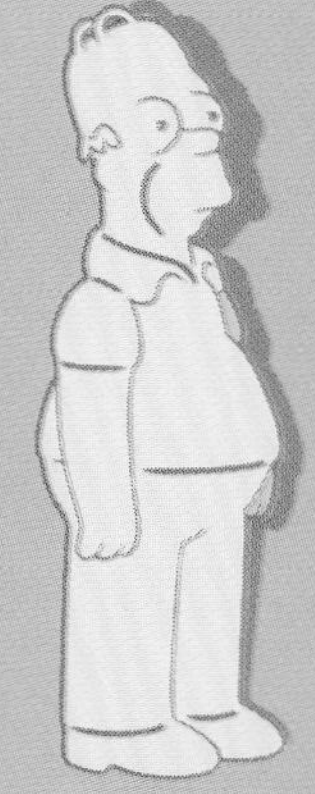

FUN FACTORY HOMER

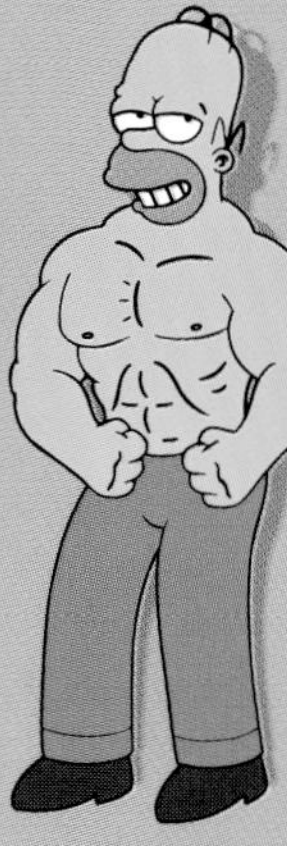

RIPPED HOMER

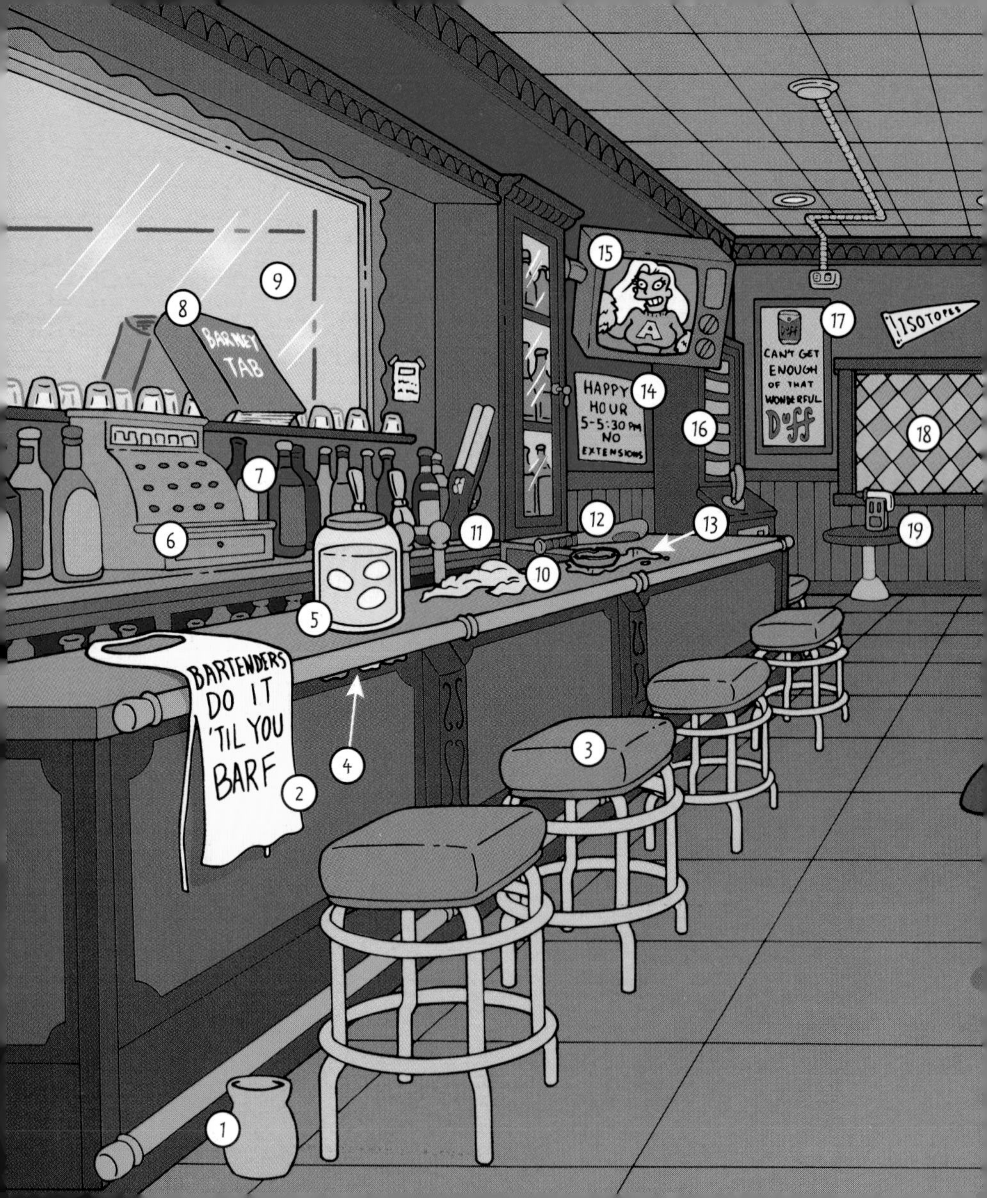
BARNEY TAB
HAPPY HOUR
5-5:30 PM
NO
EXTENSIONS
CAN'T GET
ENOUGH
OF THAT
WONDERFUL
Duff
ISOTOPES
BARTENDERS
DO IT
'TIL YOU
BARF
1
2
3
4
5
6
7
8
9
10
11
12
13
14
15
16
17
18
19

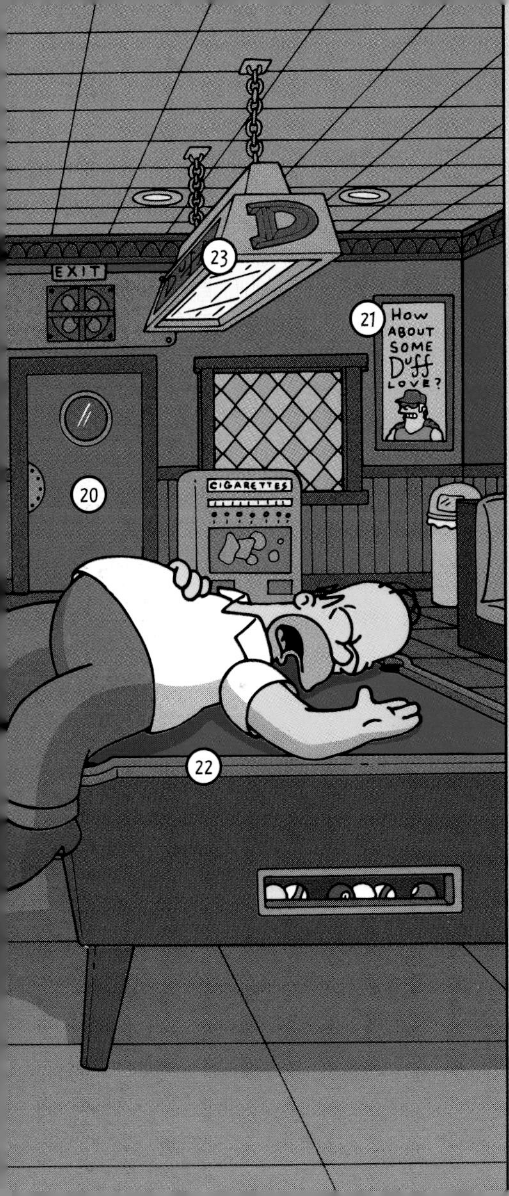
EXIT
HOW ABOUT SOME DUFF LOVE?
CIGARETTES
23
21
20
22

# HOMER'S HAUNTS
# MOE'S TAVERN

1. Spittoon.
2. Morale-building bar apron.
3. Genuine faux-Naugahyde barstools.
4. A brief history of gum (under bar rail).
5. Jar of pickled eggs (extra briny).
6. Cash register/porn-mag storage.
7. Exotic liquor bottles (strictly set dressing).
8. Barney's bar tab.
9. Mirror—Warning: People may be more inebriated than they appear.
10. Ever-present bar rag (never washed, never changed, strangely slimy).
11. Bartender's best friend.
12. Bartender's second best friend.
13. Barney's emergency beer supply
14 Cheerful sign.
15. Necessary distraction.
16. Love Tester. (How do you measure up?—Cold Fish, Luke Warm Fish, Hubba Hubba, Casanova, Hot Tamale.)
17. Motivational poster.
18. Windows (a thick greasy film prevents detection from the outside world).
19. Breathalyzer testing equipment (levels include: Tipsy, Soused, Stinkin', Boris Yeltsin).
20. Door. (Caution! During certain hours, daylight may be seep in.)
21. Inspirational poster.
22. Emergency sleeping area/tanning bed.
23. Tanning light.

# MOE SZYSLAK PROPRIETOR, MOE'S TAVERN, HOMER'S HOME AWAY FROM HOME

Gun enthusiast, and former boxer, Moe Szyslak is the proud and surly proprietor of Homer's neighborhood watering hole, Moe's Tavern. Moe's is a place where nobody knows your name and everybody wants to borrow money. Moe himself is quick to anger, desperate to please, and dynamite with the ladies—they avoid him as if their lives depended on it!

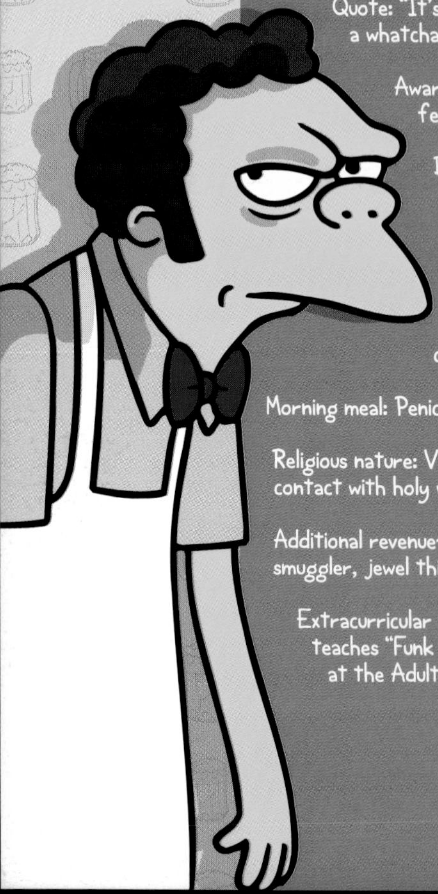

Quote: "It's been four years since my last date with a whatcha-ma-call-it...woman."

Awards and honors: Duff Days Beer-Tender of the Year, featured on the cover of "Bar and Stool" Magazine.

Birthplace: Indiana.

Current residence: Lives with his mother at 57 Walnut Street, Springfield, USA.

Physical attributes before (and after the reversal of) plastic surgery: Cauliflower ear, lizard lips, little rat eyes, caveman brow, fish snout, left-handed.

Morning meal: Penicill-O's (the Breakfast Cereal for People with Syphilis).

Religious nature: Voodoo practitioner, gambler, experienced snake handler, contact with holy water creates burning sensation.

Additional revenue-enhancing occupations: Freelance surgeon, exotic animal smuggler, jewel thief, and treasure hunter.

Extracurricular activities: Bowling, poker playing, teaches "Funk Dancing for Self-Defense" at the Adult Education Annex.

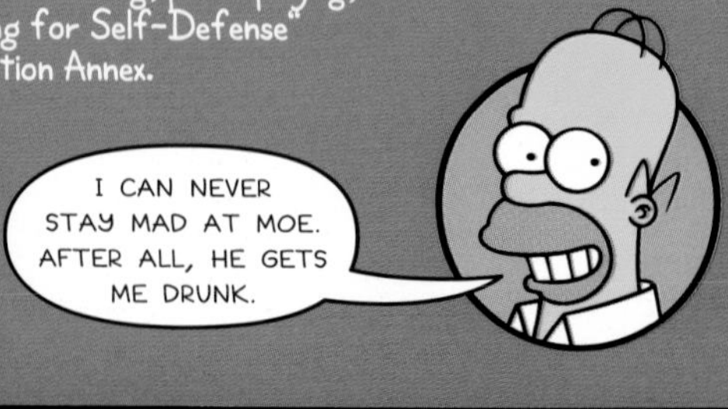
I CAN NEVER STAY MAD AT MOE. AFTER ALL, HE GETS ME DRUNK.

Barney is the most regular of regulars at Moe's Tavern. In fact, if Moe's didn't close, he'd never leave. However, Barney is not just a pathetic, belching, self-soiling alcoholic. He's also a guy who happens to love beer. Friends since high school, Homer introduced Barney to beer, thereby sparing him the indignity of an Ivy League education and the burden of steady employment.

Quote: "In case you get hungry, there's an open beer in the fridge."

Favorite color: The mesmerizing golden hue of wonderful beer.

Patriotic creed: "United States for United Statesians!"

Semi-occasionally employed as a: Department store Santa, monorail construction foreman, sneeze guard tester, Snow Plow King, horse and buggy driver, sperm donor, Krusty the Clown impersonator, clinical test subject, and float in a temperance parade.

Awards: Grammy® for "Baby on Board" as member of barbershop quartet, The Be Sharps.

Foreign attachments: Mother lives in Norway.

Musical proclivities: Lilting Irish tenor, accomplished kazoo player, musical collaboration with Linda Ronstadt on a Plow King commercial.

Film ouevre: "Pukahontas," the sensitive documentary account of his drinking difficulties.

Philanthropy: Donated $50,000 to Shelbyville Dance Theater, and once offered to make Homer an omelette.

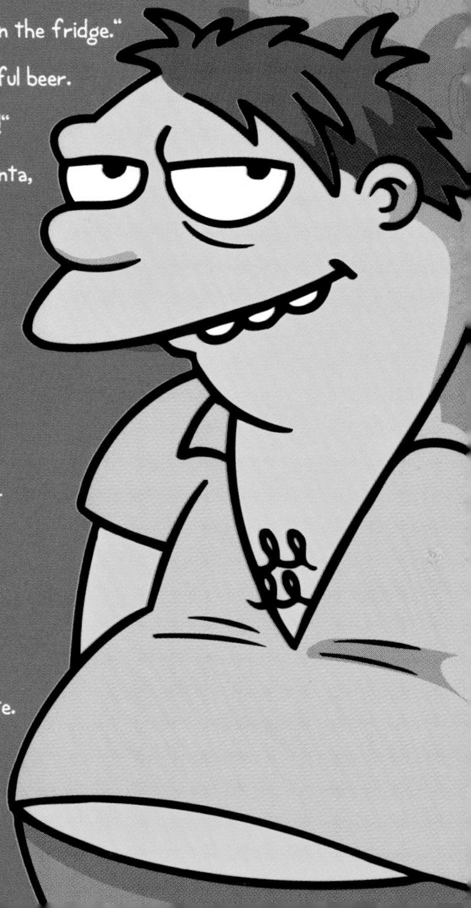

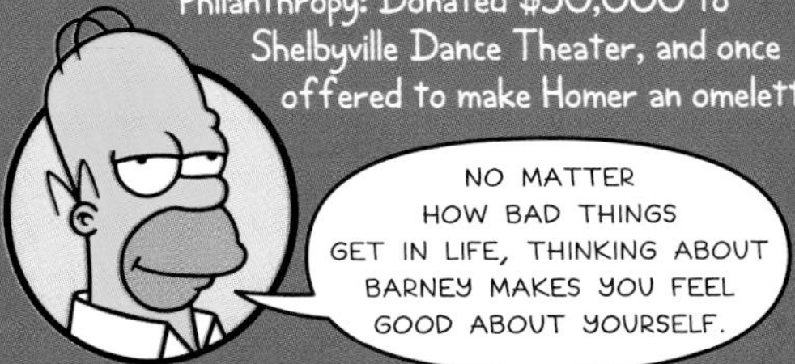
NO MATTER HOW BAD THINGS GET IN LIFE, THINKING ABOUT BARNEY MAKES YOU FEEL GOOD ABOUT YOURSELF.

# DUFFMAN THE GUY IN A COSTUME THAT CREATES AWARENESS OF DUFF

Assisted by the Duff Girls, a comely collection of costumed coquettes, Duffman brings happiness and meaning to the lives of countless couch-bound, consumer-crazed beer drinkers. By livening up their lives with his costumed capering, Duffman increases their Buy Q, so that whenever they feel a thirsty urge—they'll want some Duff.

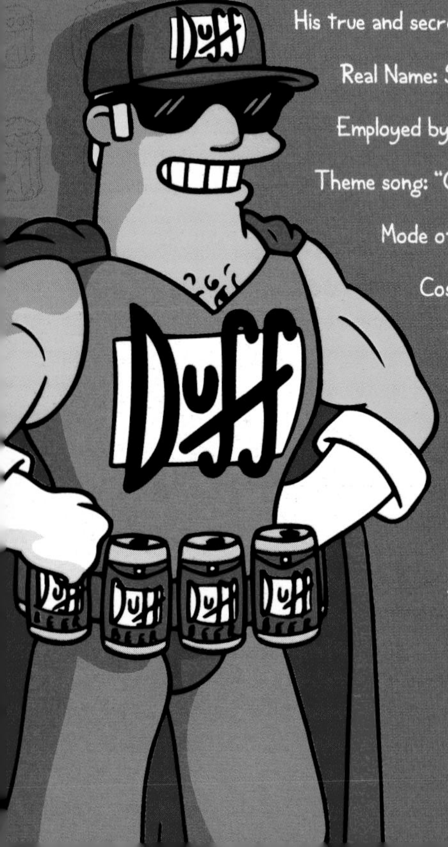

Duff
Duff
Duff
Duff
Duff
Duff


Quote: "Are you ready for some Duff love?"

His true and secret love: Doris.

Real Name: Sid. Or possibly, Larry. Or both.

Employed by: Duff Breweries, home of the world's biggest Pull Tab.

Theme song: "Oh Yeah," by Yello.

Mode of transport: The Duff Partymobile.

Costumed rival: Fuddman.

Public service: Testified before the House Subcommittee on Teenage Alcoholism.

Appearance fee: 10,000 Duff labels sent to Duff Brewery.

Types of Duff: Duff, Duff Lite, Duff Dry, Raspberry Duff, Duff Dark, Tartar-Control Duff, Lady Duff, Duff Zero, Duffahama, and Duff Gummi Beers.

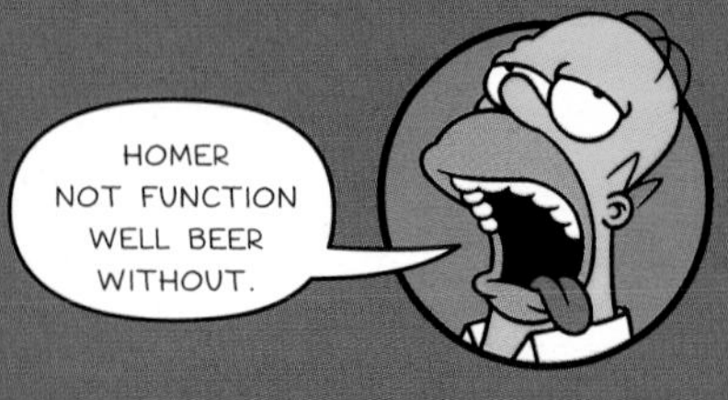

HOMER NOT FUNCTION WELL BEER WITHOUT.

Like bookends in a run-down used-paperback exchange, Sam & Larry are fixtures at Moe's Tavern—unremarkable, reliant on one another, with not much going on in between. Yet, whenever drinks are on the house, they'll be there; whenever laughter is to be had at another's expense, they'll be there; whenever encouragement is needed for some cockamamie scheme, they'll be there; but if you're looking for someone to pick up the tab...

Double Quote: "I'll have whatever he's drinking."

Their subtle yet distinct differences:

Identifying features: Sam—Hat & Glasses; Larry—Bald & Contacs.

Manner: Sam—forlorn; Larry—glum.

Pets: Sam—foxhound; Larry—hound dog.

Posture: Sam—hunchy; Larry—crunchy.

Hobbies: Sam—whittling; Larry—skittling.

Likes: Sam—Trucks with a trailer hitch and a lot of pick-up. Larry—Picking up hitchhikers in his truck.

Beer preference: Sam—Duff; Larry—Tartar-Control Duff.

Relationship with Homer: Sam—sympathizer; Larry—colleague.

THESE GUYS ARE THE GREATEST, I TELL YA. I'LL NEVER FORGET THEM, WHOEVER THEY ARE.

# LENNY & CARL HOMER'S CRONIES AND/OR ACQUAINTANCES

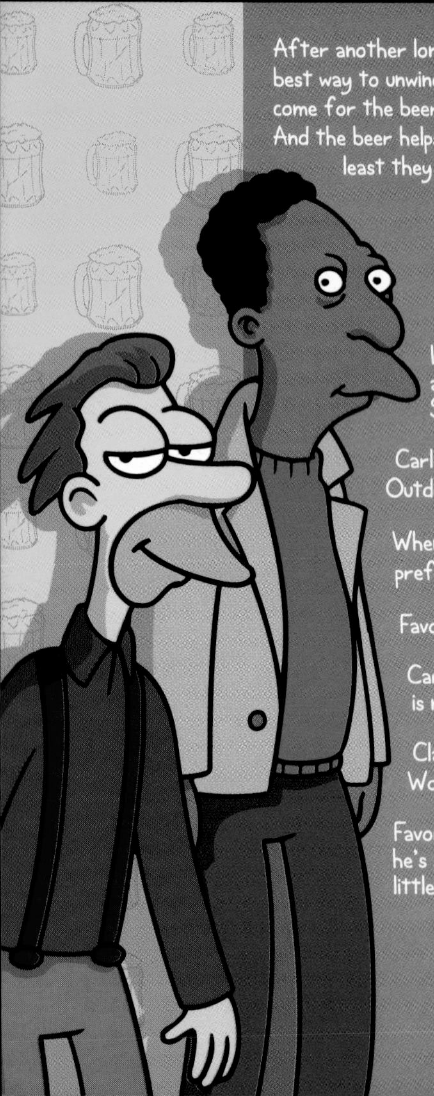

After another long day at the nuclear plant, Lenny and Carl find that the best way to unwind is hoisting an ice-cold Duff with the guys at Moe's. They come for the beer, but they stay because their home lives are so depressing. And the beer helps them forget. So they keep drinking. Well... at least they have each other. And the beer.

Quote: (Lenny) "What I did, I did because of alcohol and anger."
(Carl) "You ain't thinkin' of gettin' rid of the dank, are you Moe?

Lenny's pastimes: Teaching a class in "How to Chew Tobacco" at the Adult Education Annex, bowling, and rooting for the Springfield Isotopes.

Carl's pastimes: Clipping coupons, bowling, collecting "Men's Outdoor" magazines, and rooting for the Springfield Isotopes

When drunk: Carl wants to go to the Playboy Mansion, Lenny prefers impromptu visits to "girls colleges."

Favorite companion: Each other.

Carl takes a stand: "Any religion that embraces carob is not for Carl Carlson."

Claims to fame: Lenny was once hunted with a rifle by Rainier Wolfcastle, and Carl actually ate one of Moe's pickled eggs.

Favorite Backstreet Boy: (Carl) Nick, because he's so good to his mother. (Lenny) the little rat-faced one.

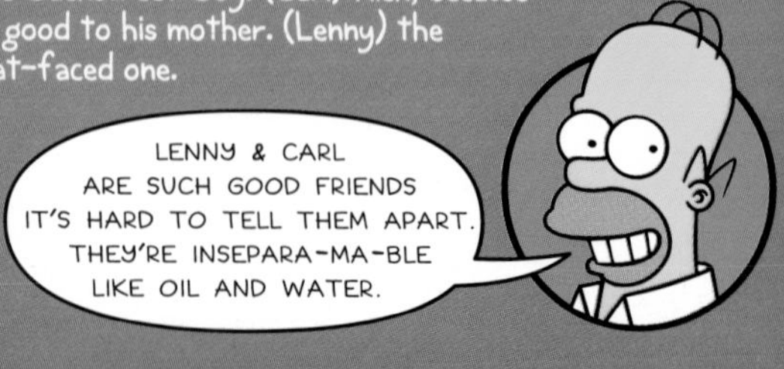
LENNY & CARL ARE SUCH GOOD FRIENDS IT'S HARD TO TELL THEM APART. THEY'RE INSEPARA-MA-BLE LIKE OIL AND WATER.

# MT. LUSHMORE

Whimsical! Urbane!
Stewed to the gills!
They're the famous
caricatures in
Moe's Tavern's
shrine to World
Class Boozers...

...MT. LUSHMORE!

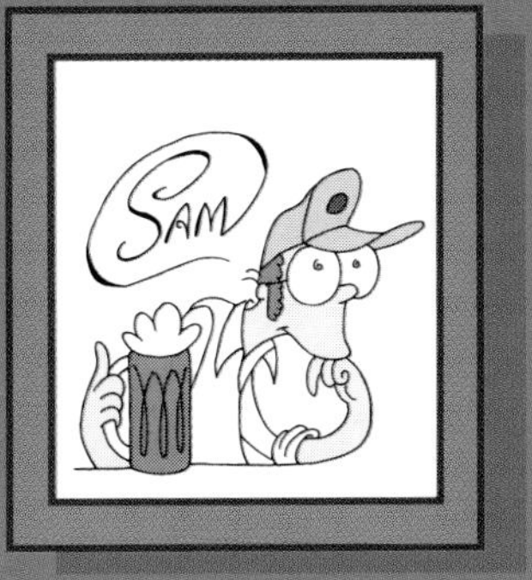
SAM

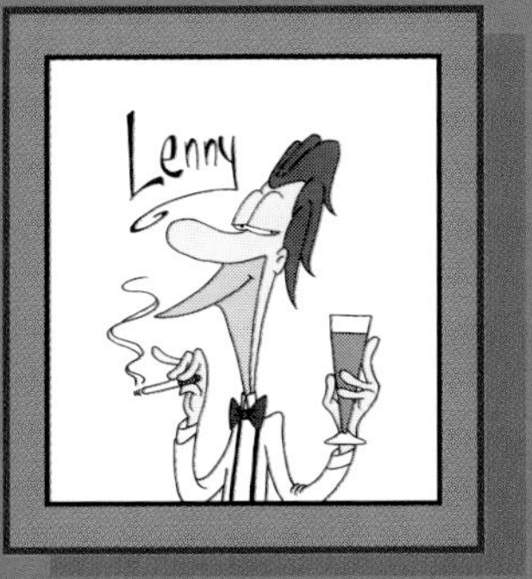
Lenny

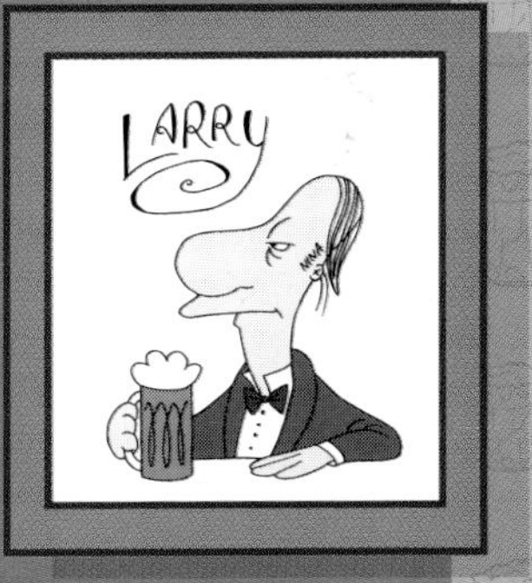
LARRY

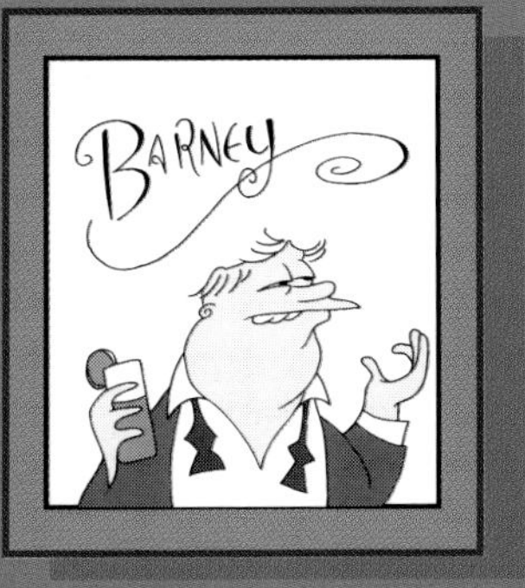
BARNEY

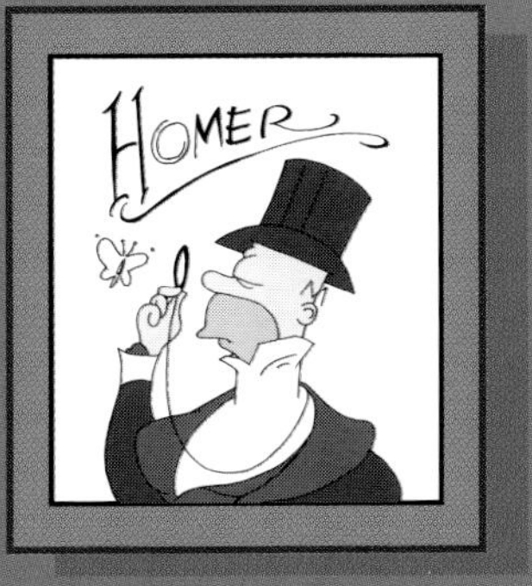
HOMER

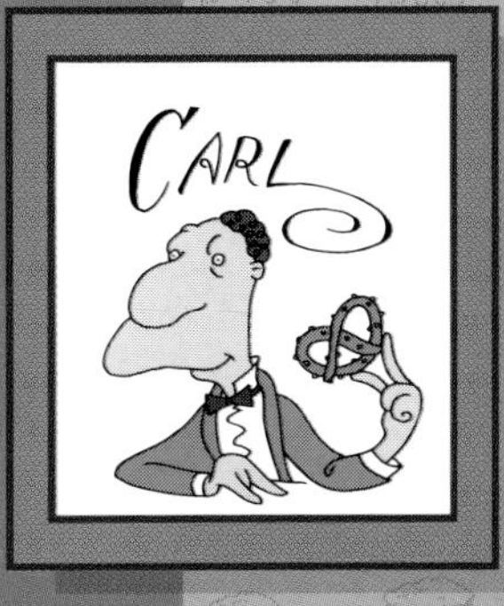
CARL

# LITTLE KNOWN FACT:

Homer's favorite song is "It's Raining Men" by the Weather Girls.

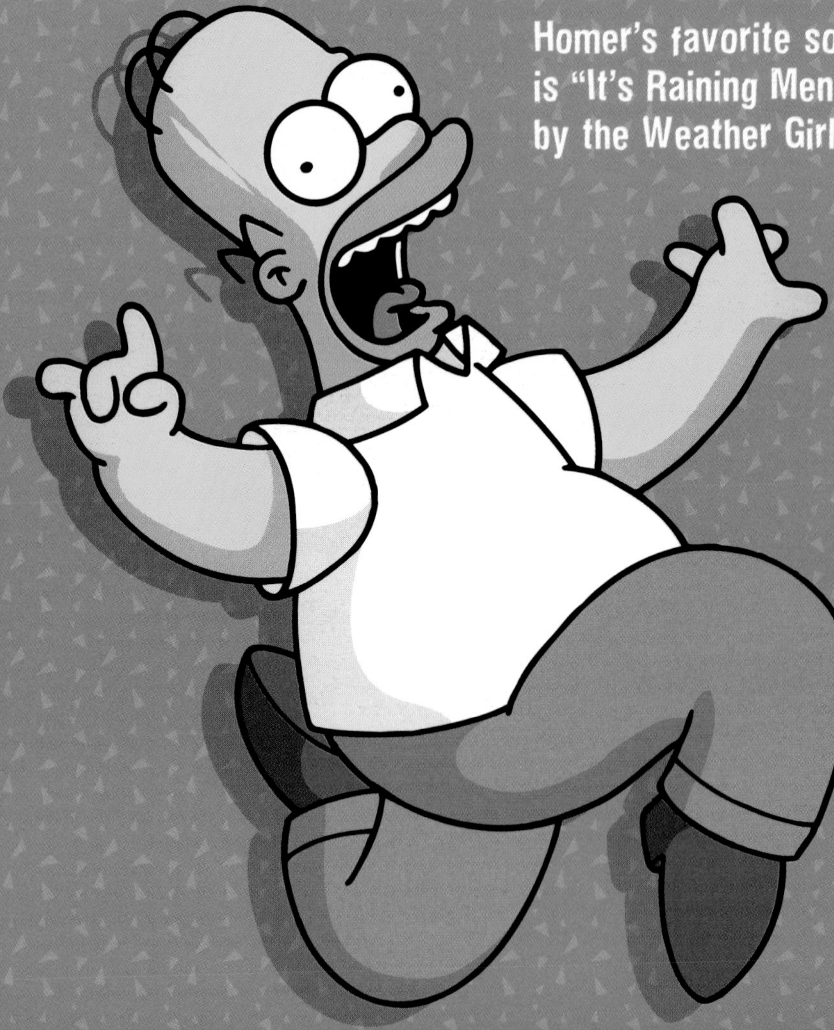

# Homer's Heroes

## BATMAN

As conductor of a runaway monorail, Homer's first choice for a savior is Batman. Sadly, he must accept help from a common non-cape-wearing scientist.

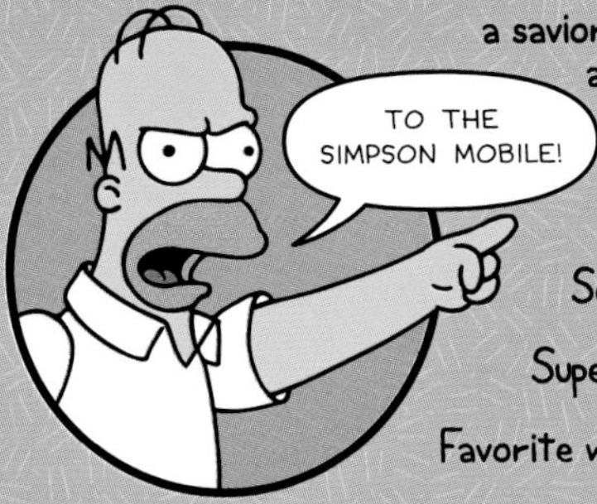
TO THE SIMPSON MOBILE!

Also known as: "The Caped Crusader," "The Dark Knight," and one half of "The Dynamic Duo."

Secret identity: Millionaire playboy Bruce Wayne.

Super powers: Despite classification as superhero—none.

Favorite weapon: The Batarang.

Choreography credit: Originator of "The Batusi."

Common misconception: Like most 5-year-olds, Homer believes Batman is a real person.

Theme song:
Na-na na-na na-na na-na,
Na-na na-na na-na na-na,
Batman!

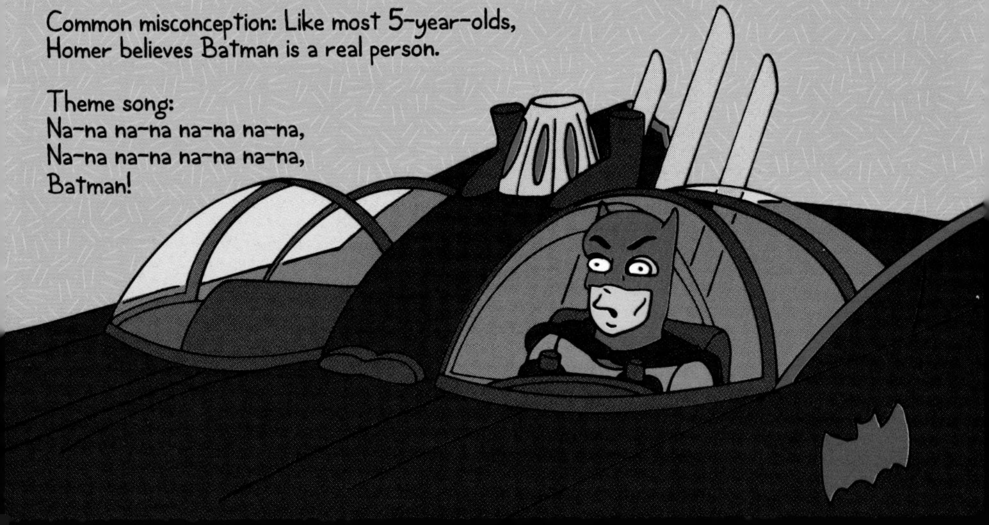

# ANATOMY OF A DIE-HARD SPORTS FAN

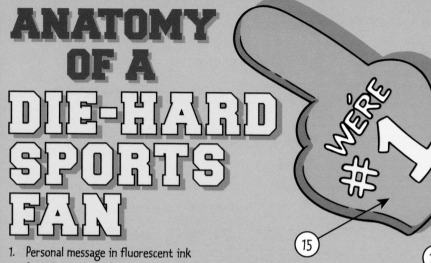

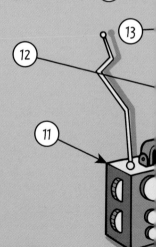

1. Personal message in fluorescent ink
2. Beer dispensing hat
3. Rainbow wig
4. Pennants of opposing team
5. Mouth-level food tray for easy hands-off gorging
6. Mustard stain
7. Beer stain
8. Binoculars
9. Giant sign with inspiring message for television viewers
10. Extra large boot tops to reclaim food & drink spillage
11. Portable radio so as not to miss play-by-play of game while distracted from actual game by food
12. Portable butt pad for maximum viewing comfort
13. Caramel corn permanently affixed to shirt
14. Humiliating plan to get on TV
15. Giant foam hand with inspiring message for team
16. Flecks of beer foam around mouth
17. Charcoal under eyes for no practical reason other than because it looks cool
18. Vein throbbing alarmingly in forehead
19. (Not pictured) Hometown Pride

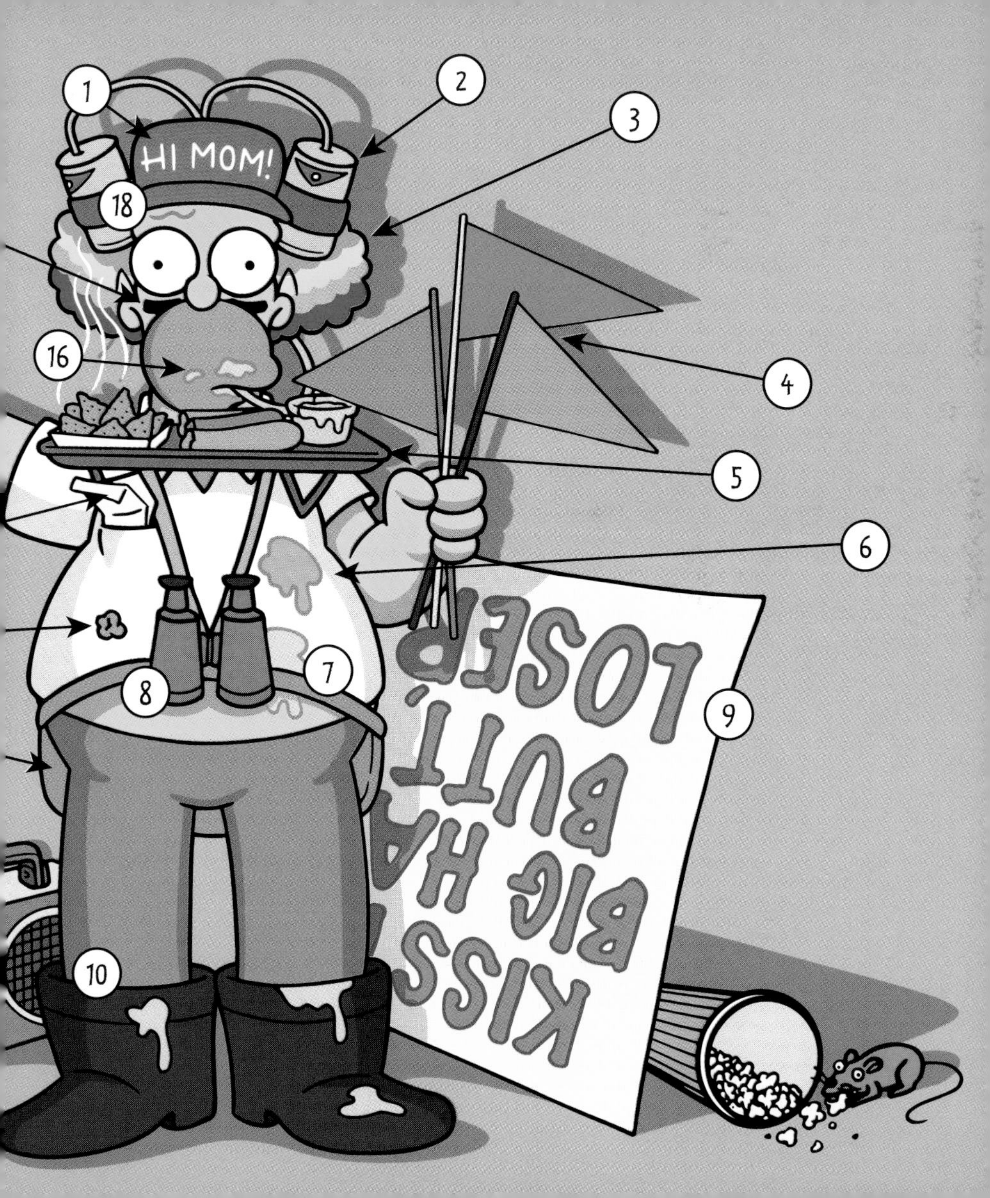
1
2
3
HI MOM!
18
16
4
5
6
7
8
9
10
KISS
BIG HA
BUTT,
LOSER

# HOMER'S Dream House

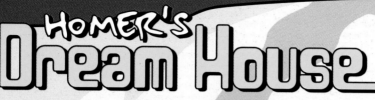

1. TAKE-OUT-THE-TRASHBOT
2. THE NACHO FOUNTAIN
3. THE ABOVE-GROUND SWIMMING POOL GROTTO (COMPLETE WITH SWIMSUIT MODELS
4. BOWLING ALLEY, (EQUIPPED FOR ROCK 'N' BOWL, MAMBO 'N' BOWL AND ACHY-BREAKY BOWL)
5. OVERSIZED BARBECUE (FOR BRONTASAURUS BURGERS!)
6. MOE'S TAVERN REPLICA (MY OWN MOE'S! COMPLETE WITH BEER NUTS AND ROBOT BARNEY, LENNY, CARL, AND MOE!)
7. SATELLITE TELE-HEAVEN (SIXTEEN TVs FOR SPORTS, BLOOPER SHOWS, AND THE "LOOK WHO'S OINKING!" DVD COLLECTION ON REPEAT)
8. GET READY TO ROCK ROOM (FOUR WALLS, A CEILING, AND A FLOOR MADE OUT OF HUGE, KICK-ASS "BACK TO THE FUTURE"-STYLE SPEAKERS! WITH A BEANBAG AND HEADPHONES!
9. THE PINCHY MEMORIAL LOBSTER TANK
10. HOLODECK
11. SPEECH BALCONY (THE BALCONY I'LL MAKE MY SPEECHES FROM)
12. THE HOMERPLEX THEATER
13. TRAMPOLINO-ROOM
14. PETTING ZOO
15. GIANT BEER SILOS
16. HELIPAD
17. ICE SCULPTING/INVENTING ROOM
18. SERVANT'S QUARTERS (WHERE MR. BURNS WILL LIVE)
19. THE ROOM OF MIRRORS THAT MAKE YOU LOOK A LOT THINNER
20. WORLD'S LONGEST SLIP 'N' SLIDE
21. ATM (FEELESS)
22. LIBRARY (COMPLETE COLLECTION OF "MAD" AND "CREEM" MAGAZINES AND "WHERE'S WALDO" BOOKS
23. ESCAPE POD
24. RUMPUS ROOM (WITH IMPORTED RUMPUS)
25. BATHROOM (WITH NEWSSTAND AND GUS, THE HAPPY-GO-LUCKY NEWSSTAND GUY)

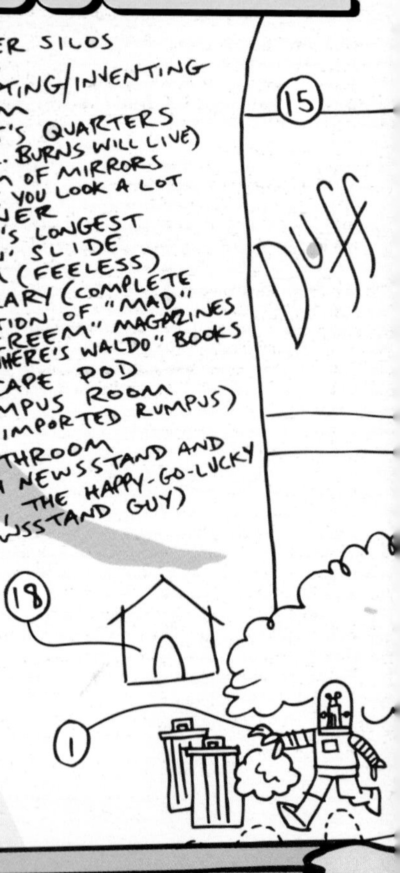

15
DUFF
18
1

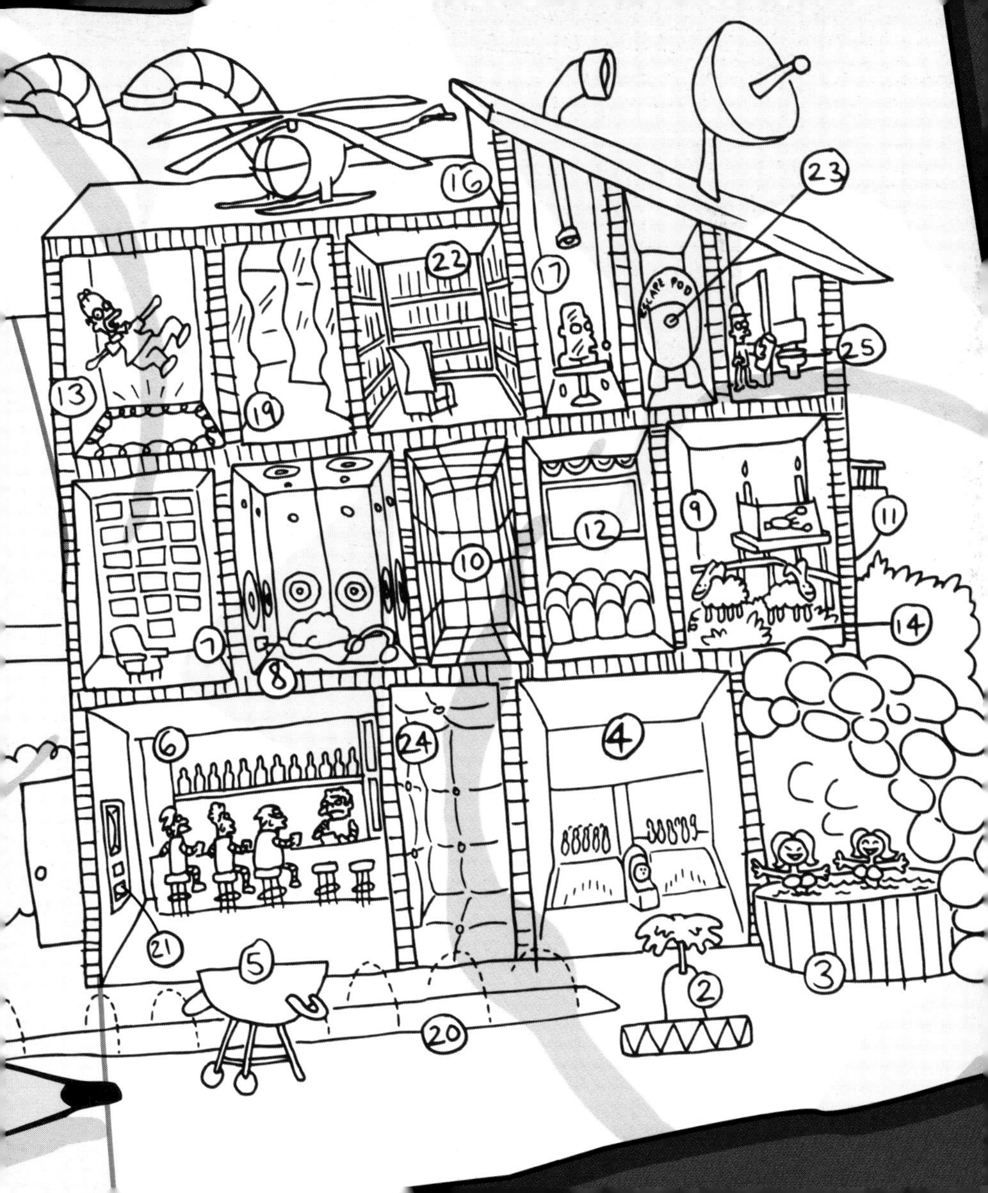

16
23
22
17
ESCAPE POD
13
19
25
9
11
12
10
7
8
14
6
24
4
21
5
2
3
20

# HOMER'S BOTTOM 40

1. Cold french fries.
2. Warm beer.
3. Alarm clocks.
4. Freakin' Flanders.
5. Still having sand between my cheeks from our beach vacation in 1997.
6. Not getting Jewish holidays off from work.
7. Broken crazy straws.
8. Taxes.
9. That Octoberfest only happens in October.
10. Hardly ever hearing "Mr. Roboto" on the radio.
11. The gruesome twosome – Patty and Selma Bouvier.
12. No hot dog venders at church.
13. Fat chicks.
14. Ten years at the nuclear power plant and still no superpowers.
15. The fact that Lynda Carter still won't answer my letters.
16. Restraining orders.
17. Having to explain why you're running down the street naked, carrying a fire hydrant.
18. WHERE THE HELL IS THE CURE FOR BALDNESS?
19. Unfunny Sunday comics.

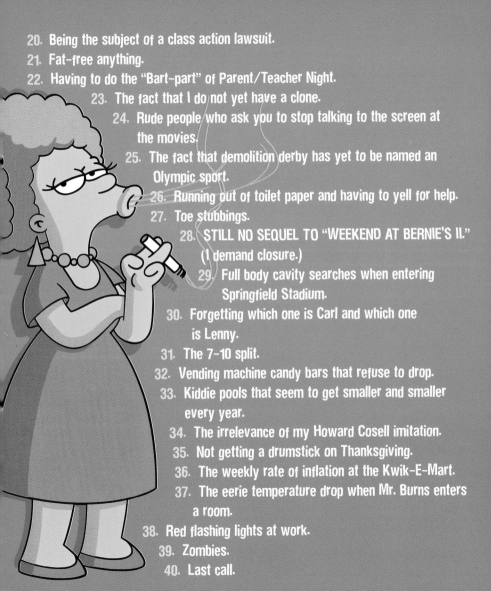

20. Being the subject of a class action lawsuit.
21. Fat-free anything.
22. Having to do the "Bart-part" of Parent/Teacher Night.
23. The fact that I do not yet have a clone.
24. Rude people who ask you to stop talking to the screen at the movies.
25. The fact that demolition derby has yet to be named an Olympic sport.
26. Running out of toilet paper and having to yell for help.
27. Toe stubbings.
28. STILL NO SEQUEL TO "WEEKEND AT BERNIE'S II." (I demand closure.)
29. Full body cavity searches when entering Springfield Stadium.
30. Forgetting which one is Carl and which one is Lenny.
31. The 7-10 split.
32. Vending machine candy bars that refuse to drop.
33. Kiddie pools that seem to get smaller and smaller every year.
34. The irrelevance of my Howard Cosell imitation.
35. Not getting a drumstick on Thanksgiving.
36. The weekly rate of inflation at the Kwik-E-Mart.
37. The eerie temperature drop when Mr. Burns enters a room.
38. Red flashing lights at work.
39. Zombies.
40. Last call.

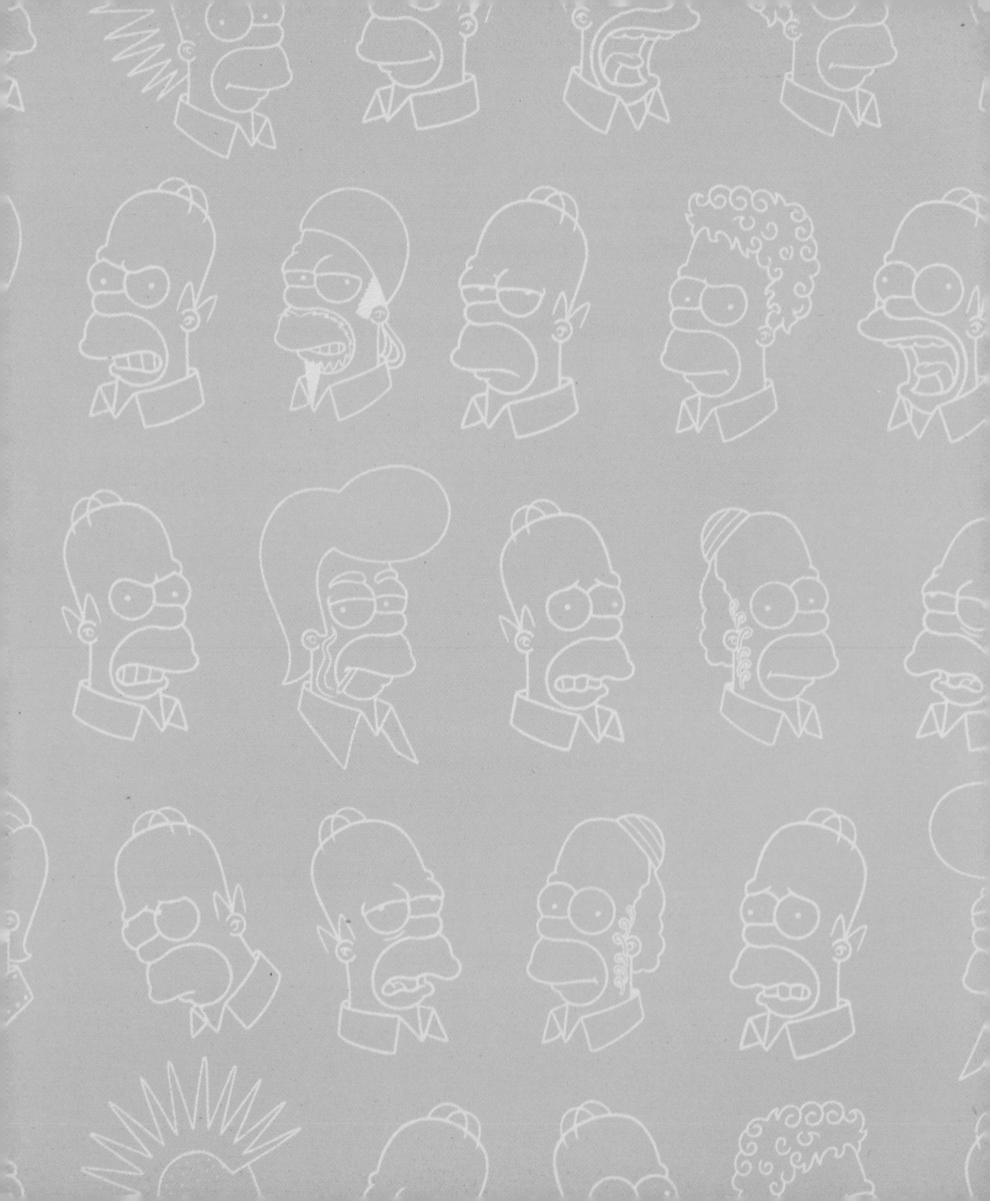